AMERICA BETWEEN THE CIVIL WAR AND THE 20TH CENTURY

1865 to 1900

DOCUMENTING AMERICA
THE PRIMARY SOURCE DOCUMENTS OF A NATION

AMERICA BETWEEN THE CIVIL WAR AND THE 20ᵀᴴ CENTURY

1865 to 1900

EDITED BY JEFF WALLENFELDT, MANAGER, GEOGRAPHY AND HISTORY

Britannica®
Educational Publishing

IN ASSOCIATION WITH

ROSEN
EDUCATIONAL SERVICES

Published in 2013 by Britannica Educational Publishing
(a trademark of Encyclopædia Britannica, Inc.)
in association with Rosen Educational Services, LLC
29 East 21st Street, New York, NY 10010.

Distributed exclusively by Rosen Educational Services.
For a listing of additional Britannica Educational Publishing titles, call toll free (800) 237-9932.

First Edition

Britannica Educational Publishing
Marilyn L. Barton: Senior Coordinator, Production Control
Steven Bosco: Director, Editorial Technologies
Lisa S. Braucher: Senior Producer and Data Editor
Yvette Charboneau: Senior Copy Editor
Kathy Nakamura: Manager, Media Acquisition
Jeff Wallenfeldt: Manager, Geography and History

Rosen Educational Services
Jeanne Nagle: Senior Editor
Nelson Sá: Art Director
Cindy Reiman: Photography Manager
Brian Garvey: Designer, Cover Design
Introduction by Jeff Wallenfeldt

Library of Congress Cataloging-in-Publication Data

America Between the Civil War and the 20th century, 1865 to 1900/edited by Jeff
Wallenfeldt.—1st ed.
     p. cm. -- (Documenting America--the primary source documents of a nation)
Includes bibliographical references and index.
ISBN 978-1-61530-684-8 (library binding)
1. United States—History—1865–1898—Sources. I. Wallenfeldt, Jeffrey H.
E173.A46 2012
973.8—dc23

2011049631

Manufactured in the United States of America

On the cover: Detail of the Sherman Anti-Trust Act of 1890. *National Archives and Records
Administration, Washington, D.C.;* A stagecoach traveling across the American frontier in
the 1880s. Westward expansion was but one of the hallmarks of growth in the United States
between the Civil War and the 20th century. *Time & Life Pictures/Getty Images*

On pages viii-ix: Members of the Illinois National Guard stationed in the rail yards during
the 1894 Pullman Railroad strike. Battles between owners and labour unions were common
at this time. *Chicago History Museum/Archive Photos/Getty Images*

On pages 1, 8, 15, 23, 30, 34, 39, 44, 51, 61: Illustration highlighting the Champion light steel
hay binder. Industry soon surpassed agriculture as a leading economic factor in America after
the Civil War. *Buyenlarge/Archive Photos/Getty Images*

CONTENTS

4

6

26

64

66

66

In the middle of the 19th century the United States was so polarized, particularly by the issue of slavery, that it fought a great civil war, leaving the states of the former Confederacy economically devastated while many states that had remained loyal to the Union rushed headlong into the industrial future. Even as the country sought to bind up its wounds, it remained a land of dichotomous contrasts on matters of ideology and economics that became increasingly stark as the 19th century pushed to its close. The familiar division of North and South remained, but, more than ever, the competing interests of urban and rural America came to the fore, as did those of the rich and the poor, whose class warfare was most often fought in battles between organized labour and corporate ownership. Moreover, the social landscape of the United States was changing almost as fast as the rapidly developing technology that was transforming the economy.

The best way to get a sense of the magnitude of these changes is in the words of those who experienced them in the moment, whether they stood at the centre shaping events or on the periphery being shaped by them. The primary source documents in this volume, which range from speeches and songs to legislation and literature, open a window on the world of the United States in the last third of the 19th century. Those documents and the narrative history through which they are interwoven work as a grand mural that offers both the long view of history, dominated by broad strokes, and the short view, where readers may examine evocative details. Shorter documents are presented in their entirety. More often, however, excerpts are provided that give a flavour of the document, which is presented more fully in the Appendix. Specific introductions for each document provide additional context.

The population of the United States expanded exponentially between the Civil War and the 20th century, largely as a result of the increasing influx of immigrants. Americans' response to immigration during this period varied from an open-armed boosterism grounded in the optimism of the Constitution to xenophobic rejection that sprung from the fear of losing jobs to new immigrants and ugly racism. Presented to the United States by France and dedicated in 1886, the Statue of Liberty towered over Ellis Island, the point of entry for millions seeking a better life. "Give me your tired, your poor,/Your huddled masses yearning to breathe free,/The wretched refuse of your teeming shore," poet Emma Lazarus wrote in her inscription for the statue's pedestal. Yet earlier in the same decade the Chinese Exclusion Act prohibited Chinese immigration because "in the opinion of the government of the United States the coming of Chinese laborers to this country endangers the good order of certain localities." This was the prevailing sentiment even after Chinese "coolies" had contributed mightily to the building of the Central Pacific Railroad that joined with the Union Pacific in Utah in 1869 to form a transcontinental railroad.

The proliferation of railroads throughout the country was a hallmark national achievement celebrated in songs such as "John Henry," the story a legendary "steel-driving" railworker whose hammer made "cold steel ring." The expanding network of railroads helped close distances in a big country that got even bigger with the purchase of Alaska from Russia in 1867. Seen as frivolous by many Americans at the time, the acquisition was lampooned as Seward's Folly. But Secretary of State William Seward, who negotiated the purchase, would have the last laugh—not only because of Alaska's natural beauty (which Seward described as surpassing "in sublimity that of either the Alps, the Appenines, the Alleghenies, or the Rocky Mountains") but also because of it mineral wealth.

Migration westward remained a defining characteristic of American life. Gold strikes made California and western locations magnets for itinerant dreamers. When a vein was exhausted, the exodus could be rapid, leaving behind ghost towns. Often, though, the futile search for gold resulted in discoveries of silver, resulting in more-enduring communities that lacked nothing in the way of local colour or get-rich-quick schemers. In a letter to his brother in 1869, Henry Eno wrote, "We have here...numbers too lazy to work but not too lazy to steal, and some too proud to work and not afraid to steal."

The movement west almost always came at the expense of Native Americans, displaced to reservations on less desirable land. Of the native people of Alaska Seward said, they "will do here as they seem to have done in Washington Territory and British Colombia—they will merely serve their turn until civilized white men come." Seward was out of office at the time, but his characterization was not far from the de facto government stance cloaked by the official Indian policy. Chief Joseph of the Nez Percé people, who were coerced off their land in Oregon to make way for miners and settlers, had little faith in the government's Indian policy or those who implemented it: "This talk fell like a heavy stone upon my heart....Other law chiefs [congressional committees] came to see me and said they would help me to get a healthy country. I did not know who to believe."

By 1889 even large tracts of the Oklahoma Territory, the land known as Indian Territory, were opened for settlement. The promise of 160 acres of free land resulted in the chaotic land rush that participant Hamilton S. Wicks wrote "was not over when you reached the particular lot you were content to select for your possession. The contest still was who should drive their stakes first, who would erect their little tents soonest, and then who would quickest build a little wooden shanty."

A select few amassed huge fortunes during the explosive growth of American industry and technology. John P. Morgan made tens of millions in finance, John D. Rockefeller in oil, and Andrew Carnegie in the manufacture of steel. For all of his business acumen, Carnegie saw his primary interest as arts and letters; his charitable giving continued to provide for the arts into the 21st century. Though he was not alone among the so-called Captains of Industry in his philanthropic largesse, Carnegie also shared his vision in articles he wrote for periodicals. "To reach her proper position and play her part among the nations," Carnegie wrote of the United States in one such article, "she must not only be the wealthiest country in the world but richest in the diffusion of refinement and culture among the people."

Despite their philanthropy, these wealthy industrialists were anything but universally admired, for not only had they made their fortunes by consolidating competing firms into large cooperative units called trusts that dominated whole industries, but also many believed they had done so on the backs of workers. Noting that the change from competition to combination was "nothing less than one of those revolutions which march through history with giant strides," journalist Henry Demarest Lloyd concluded, "we have given competition its own way and have found that we are not good enough or wise enough to be trusted with this power of ruining ourselves in the attempt to ruin others."

Laissez-faire capitalism provided the titans of industry with the upper hand in American society. Yet as organized labour grew in the last half of the 19th century, unions fought to keep workers from under the thumb of owners and managers, seeking fair wages and safer workplaces, an eight-hour day, and an end to child labour. Adopted in 1878, the constitution of the Knights of Labor warned that the aggregation of wealth in the hands of the few would "invariably lead to the pauperization and hopeless degradation of the toiling masses...that a check should be placed upon its power and upon unjust accumulation, and a system adopted which will secure to the laborer the fruits of his toil." Strikes were the unions' principal weapon; in 1886 alone there 1,600 of them. That year is also remembered for the Haymarket Riot, where a bomb of uncertain origin that killed seven policeman was blamed on anarchist agitators. Unionism was badly tarnished by its association with the event in the popular mind.

In 1894, near Chicago, a landmark strike pitted the men who made railroad cars against the company's owner, George Pullman, who had cut wages but refused to reduce the rent on the homes he had built for his workers. "He hopes to starve us out...and to deduct from our miserable wages when we are forced to return to him the last dollar we owe him for the occupancy of his houses," the strikers wrote in a position statement. At the time of the Pullman strike Samuel Gompers, president of American Federation Labor, maintained that "the laborers must learn to think and act, and soon, too, that only by the power of organization and common concert of action can...their rights to life (work to sustain it) be recognized, and liberty and rights secured." Ironically, the Sherman Antitrust Act, enacted in 1890 in an attempt to curb the growth of corporate monopolies, was used against the unions with claims that their actions violated the act's prohibition on "conspiracy in the restraint of trade."

At this moment, when strong guidance from the White House would have been invaluable, there was instead a string of less than stellar presidents, or so thought future president Woodrow Wilson, still an academic, in 1885. Wilson believed that Congress had grown too powerful. "I am inclined to think," he wrote, "that the decline in the character of Presidents is not the cause but only the accompanying manifestation of the declining prestige of the presidential office. That high office has fallen from its first estate of dignity because its power has waned." One of those presidents, Rutherford B. Hayes, who unlike most Republicans opposed trusts, took a stronger stand out of office than in, when he wrote "the giant evil and danger in this country, the danger which transcends all others is the vast wealth owned or controlled by a few persons." Grover

Cleveland, the only president who served discontinuous terms, sought to make his mark by lowering the tariff. "Our present tariff laws, the vicious, inequitable, and illogical source of unnecessary taxation ought to be at once revised and amended," he said in his annual message to Congress in 1887.

Notwithstanding the surplus in the federal coffers at the time of Cleveland's address and the ostentatious displays of luxury by the wealthy few, the Gilded Age (Mark Twain and Charles Dudley Warner's name for the period) was also a time of financial panics and economic depressions. Jacob Coxey, who led an "army" in a march on Washington in 1894 to demand action, called on the government to mount public works projects to mitigate the economic suffering, and to pay for it by the printing of "$500 million of Treasury notes." The hard times experienced by farmers in the West resulted in an explosion of political activism and organizing in the 1890s. The Grange had already played an important role in bringing about the enactment of the Interstate Commerce Act to regulate the railroads. In writing about the Grange and the Farmers' Alliance, Sen. William A. Peffer of Kansas noted their observance of gender equity: "These social bodies of farmers...are fast, very fast, educating the rural mind to the belief that women are as necessary in public affairs as they are in private affairs."

Farmers' organizations such as these became the backbone of the populist movement, which advocated government ownership of the railroads, the imposition of an income tax, expansion of the money supply, and a "free silver" policy, under which currency would be redeemable for either gold or silver. The matter of a bimetallic standard versus a gold standard became perhaps the single greatest issue of the day. On one side, critics of free silver (generally Republicans), such as economist James Laurence Laughlin, believed that the free coinage of silver (at a rate of 16 to 1 for gold) was "a huge deceit...born in the private offices of the sliver kings, nursed and the hands of speculators, clothed in economic error." On the other side were most Democrats and the Populists, whose most eloquent advocate was William Jennings Bryan, their presidential candidate in 1896, who,

in his famous "Cross of Gold" speech, defended the coinage of silver as egalitarian. "There are two ideas of government," he said. "There are those who believe that if you just legislate to make the well-to-do prosperous that their prosperity will leak through on those below. The Democratic idea has been that if you legislate to make the masses prosperous their prosperity will find its way up and through every class that rests upon it."

Herein lies not only the epitome of the stark ideological clashes that characterized the period, but, in Bryan's description of "trickle-down" economic theory, a reminder that some of the arguments of the late 19th century remain at the heart of American political discourse today.

CHAPTER 1

GROWTH OF THE COUNTRY

During the decades between the end of the Civil War and the beginning of the 20th century, the United States expanded to include all of the states that currently constitute the union, save for New Mexico, Arizona, and Oklahoma, which were U.S. territories (the last as Indian Territory) by the end of the war, and Alaska and Hawaii, which were acquired by the United States by the turn of the century. Nine states joined the Union during the period: Nebraska (1867), Colorado (1876), North and South Dakota, Montana, and Washington (all 1889), Idaho and Wyoming (both 1890), and Utah (1896). The population of the continental United States in 1880 was slightly above 50 million. In 1900 it was just under 76 million—a gain of more than 50 percent, but still the smallest rate of population increase for any 20-year period of the 19th century. The rate of growth was unevenly distributed, ranging from less than 10 percent in northern New England to more than 125 percent in the 11 states and territories of the Far West. Most of the states east of the Mississippi reported gains slightly below the national average.

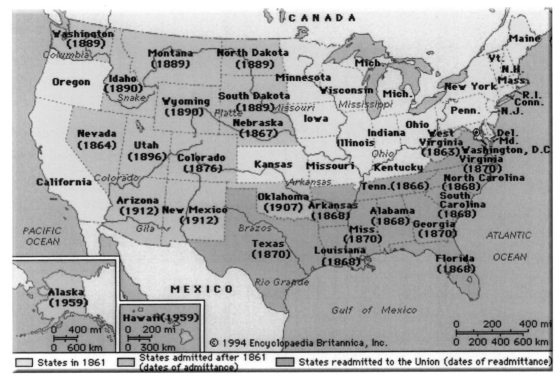

The United States after 1861. Encyclopædia Britannica, Inc.

IMMIGRATION

Much of the population increase was due to the more than 9 million immigrants who entered the United States in the last 20 years of the century, the largest number to arrive in any comparable period up to that time. From the earliest days of the republic until 1895, the majority of immigrants had come from northern or western Europe. Beginning in 1896, however, the great majority of the immigrants were from southern or eastern Europe.

Notwithstanding the welcoming hand extended by some Americans, other nervous Americans, already convinced that immigrants wielded too much political power or were responsible for violence and industrial strife, found new cause for alarm, fearing that the new immigrants could not easily be assimilated into American society. Those fears gave added stimulus to agitation for legislation limiting the number of immigrants eligible for admission to the United States, and in the early 20th century led to quota laws favouring immigrants from northern and western Europe.

Until that time, the only major restriction against immigration was the Chinese Exclusion Act, passed by Congress in 1882, prohibiting for a period of 10 years

Document: Emma Lazarus: "The New Colossus" (1886)

Emma Lazarus's precocity as a poet brought her works public attention when she was age 18, but her interest in her Jewish heritage was slower to develop and lay dormant until she learned of the 1879–83 Russian pogroms against the Jews. When Jewish refugees began arriving in the United States in 1881, Lazarus organized relief programs and published a bitter attack on the pogroms in Century Magazine. *The last five lines of her sonnet, "The New Colossus," were selected for inscription on the pedestal of the Statue of Liberty, dedicated Oct. 28, 1886.*

Source: *Poems*, Boston, 1889, Vol. II.

THE NEW COLOSSUS

Not like the brazen giant of Greek fame,
With conquering limbs astride from land to land;
Here at our sea-washed, sunset gates shall stand
A mighty woman with a torch, whose flame
Is the imprisoned lightning, and her name
Mother of Exiles. From her beacon-hand
Glows world-wide welcome; her mild eyes command
The air-bridged harbor that twin cities frame.
"Keep, ancient lands, your storied pomp!" cries she
With silent lips. "Give me your tired, your poor,
Your huddled masses yearning to breathe free,
The wretched refuse of your teeming shore.
Send these, the homeless, tempest-tossed to me:
I lift my lamp beside the golden door!"

the immigration of Chinese labourers into the United States. This act was both the culmination of more than a decade of agitation on the West Coast for the exclusion of the Chinese and an early sign of the coming change in the traditional U.S. philosophy of welcoming virtually all immigrants.

The Chinese Exclusion Act was renewed in 1892 for another 10-year period. In 1902 the suspension of Chinese immigration was made indefinite.

WESTWARD MIGRATION

The United States completed its North American expansion in 1867, when Secretary of State William H. Seward persuaded Congress to purchase Alaska from Russia.

Striking coal miners attacking Chinese labourers. Fearing that Asian immigrants would take American jobs and cause civil unrest, Congress enacted the Chinese Exclusion Act of 1882. MPI/Archive Photos/Getty Images

Document: The Chinese Exclusion Act (1882)

By 1882 approximately 375,000 Chinese had immigrated to the United States, nearly all on the West Coast. The Burlingame Treaty of 1868 provided for unlimited immigration but denied the Chinese the right of citizenship. During the early 1870s an economic depression and the massing of cheap "coolie" labor in West Coast cities gave rise to fierce economic competition with American workers, whose demand for higher wages put them at a disadvantage. Fearing civil disorder, Congress in 1879 passed an act restricting Chinese immigration; Pres. Rutherford B. Hayes vetoed it on the grounds that it violated the Burlingame Treaty. In 1880 the treaty was revised to limit Chinese labor immigration, and on May 6, 1882, Congress passed the Chinese Exclusion Act.

Whereas, in the opinion of the government of the United States the coming of Chinese laborers to this country endangers the good order of certain localities within the territory thereof; therefore,

Be it enacted by the Senate and House of Representatives of the United States of America in Congress assembled, that from and after the expiration of ninety days next after the passage of this act, and until the expiration of ten years next after the passage of this act, the coming of Chinese laborers to the United States be, and the same is hereby, suspended; and during such suspension it shall not be lawful for any Chinese laborer to come, or, having so come after the expiration of said ninety days, to remain within the United States.

Section 2. That the master of any vessel who shall knowingly bring within the United States on such vessel, and land or permit to be landed, any Chinese laborer from any foreign port or place shall be deemed guilty of a misdemeanor, and on conviction thereof shall be punished by a fine of not more than $500 for each and every such Chinese laborer so brought, and may be also imprisoned for a term not exceeding one year....

Document: William H. Seward: The Promise of Alaska (1869)

The idea of purchasing Alaska from Russia had been discussed as early as 1859, but the Civil War hindered any useful negotiations. Commercial interests on the West Coast were especially desirous of obtaining fishing and trading rights in the territory, which was governed by the Russian-American Company, a commercial monopoly that ruled Alaska on behalf of the Russian imperial government. Because the company's monopoly was unprofitable, and the territory was too distant from St. Petersburg to be governed or protected adequately, the Russian minister to Washington conferred in March 1867 with Secretary of State William H. Seward over the possible purchase of Alaska by the United States. Seward, always an ardent expansionist, eagerly negotiated a treaty that was ratified by the Senate on April 9. The United States paid $7.2 million for what came to be called "Seward's Folly" or "Seward's Arctic Province." After Seward left office he made a world tour that included a visit to Alaska to see his purchase firsthand. On Aug. 12, 1869, he made the following speech at Sitka in southeastern Alaska, in which he looked forward to the time when Alaska would take its place as a state in the Union.

Citizens of Alaska, Fellow Citizens of the United States:

You have pressed me to meet you in public assembly once before I leave Alaska. It would be sheer affectation to pretend to doubt your sincerity in making this request, and capriciously ungrateful to refuse it, after having received so many and varied hospitalities from all sorts and conditions of men. It is not an easy task, however, to speak in a manner worthy of your consideration while I am living constantly on shipboard, as you all know, and am occupied intently in searching out whatever is sublime, or beautiful, or peculiar, or useful.

On the other hand, it is altogether natural on your part to say, "You have looked upon Alaska; what do you think of it?" Unhappily, I have seen too little of Alaska to answer the question satisfactorily. The entire coastline of the United States, exclusive of Alaska, is 10,000 miles, while the coastline of Alaska alone, including the islands, is 26,000 miles. The portion of the territory which lies east of the peninsula, including islands, is 120 miles wide. The western portion, including Aleutian Islands, expands to a breadth of 2,200 miles. The entire land area, including islands, is 577,390 statute square miles.

We should think a foreigner very presumptuous who should presume to give the world an opinion of the whole of the United States of America after he had merely looked in from his steamer at Plymouth and Boston Harbor, or had run up the Hudson River to the Highlands, or had ascended the Delaware to Trenton, or the James River to Richmond, or the Mississippi no farther than Memphis. My observation thus far has hardly been more comprehensive....

Thereafter, the development of the West progressed rapidly, with the percentage of American citizens living west of the Mississippi increasing from about 22 percent in 1880 to 27 percent in 1900. New states were added to the Union throughout the century. By 1900 there were only three territories still awaiting statehood in the continental United States: Oklahoma, Arizona, and New Mexico.

Painting of settlers during the western U.S. land rush in the Oklahoma Territory in the late 1880s. In the last decades of the 19th century, land west of the Mississippi experienced a tremendous population surge. MPI/Archive Photos/Getty Images

URBAN GROWTH

In 1890 the Bureau of the Census discovered that a continuous line could no longer be drawn across the West to define the farthest advance of settlement. Despite the continuing westward movement of population, the frontier had become a symbol of the past. The movement of people from farms to cities more accurately predicted the trends of the future. In 1880 about 28 percent of the American people lived in communities designated by the Bureau of the Census as urban; by 1900 that figure had risen to 40 percent. In those statistics could be read the beginning of the decline of rural power in America and the emergence of a society built upon a burgeoning industrial complex.

CHAPTER 2

THE WEST

Abraham Lincoln once described the West as the "treasure house of the nation." In the 30 years after the discovery of gold in California, prospectors found gold or silver in every state and territory of the far West.

THE MINERAL EMPIRE

There were few truly rich "strikes" in the post-Civil War years. Of those few, the most important were the fabulously rich Comstock Lode of silver in western Nevada (first discovered in 1859 but developed more extensively later) and the discovery of gold in the Black Hills of South Dakota (1874) and at Cripple Creek, Colo. (1891).

Each new discovery of gold or silver produced an instant mining town to supply the needs and pleasures of the prospectors. If most of the ore was close to the surface, the prospectors would soon extract it and depart, leaving behind a ghost town—empty of people but a reminder of a romantic moment in the past. If the veins ran deep, organized groups with the capital to buy the needed machinery would move in to mine the subsoil wealth, and the mining town would gain some stability as the centre of a local industry. In a few

A cutaway section of a hillside showing activity inside the mines of the Comstock Lode. Library of Congress Prints and Photographs Division

Document: Henry Eno: Silver in Nevada (1869)

During the three decades following the Civil War wave after wave of pioneers swept over the Missouri River, bent on gaining wealth in the new Western territories. The miners were first on the scene, and, after their disappointment when the California gold rush of 1849 subsided, many headed East again and found rich gold and silver deposits in Nevada and Colorado. Usually, as with the case of the fabulous Comstock Lode at the Ophir mine, Nevada, prospectors were looking for gold and found silver as an accidental by-product of this search. Henry Eno, who was present at the height of Nevada's fame as mining territory, wrote to his brother William on Aug. 21, 1869, describing the activity at Hamilton White Pine.

Dear Brother:

Yours of the 11th August was received yesterday. Have now been here since the 3rd of July. I came here expecting to find a rich mineral country, also to find much such a population as California had in 1849 and '50. The great mineral wealth of eastern Nevada has not been exaggerated. In fact I did not expect to find so rich or so many silver mines. There is not so much wild reckless extravagance among the people of the towns and the miners as in the early days of California. There are not as many homicides according to the numbers, but there is perhaps more highway robberies committed. We have here, as twenty years ago, numbers too lazy to work but not too lazy to steal, and some too proud to work and not afraid to steal. The laws of Nevada license gambling, and here at Hamilton, in Treasure City, and Shermantown are some ten or twelve licensed gambling tables. The next session of the legislature may perhaps license highway robbery.

There are two banking establishments, two express offices. Wells Fargo and Union Express, some ten or twelve assay offices, and a small army of lawyers. The District Court has been in session ever since I arrived. A trial often occupies ten or twelve days. A very few lawyers are doing well. From what I can discover I believe that lawyers depend more upon perjury and subornation of perjury than upon principles of law or precedents. Experts in mining do a thriving business as witnesses....

instances, those towns gained permanent status as the commercial centres of agricultural areas that first developed to meet the needs of the miners but later expanded to produce a surplus that they exported to other parts of the West.

THE OPEN RANGE

At the close of the Civil War, the price of beef in the Northern states was abnormally high. At the same time, millions of cattle grazed aimlessly on the plains of Texas. A few shrewd Texans concluded that there might be greater profits in cattle than in cotton, especially because it required little capital to enter the cattle business—only enough to employ a few cowboys to tend the cattle during the year and to drive them to market in the spring. No one owned the cattle, and they grazed without charge upon the public domain.

The one serious problem was the shipment of the cattle to market. The Kansas Pacific resolved that problem when it completed a rail line that ran as far west as Abilene, Kan., in 1867. Abilene was 200 miles (300 kilometres) from the nearest point in Texas where the cattle grazed during the year, but Texas cattlemen almost immediately instituted the annual practice of driving that portion of their herds that was ready for market overland to Abilene in the spring. There they met representatives of Eastern packinghouses, to whom they sold their cattle.

The open-range cattle industry prospered beyond expectations and even attracted capital from conservative investors in the British Isles. By the 1880s the industry had expanded along the plains as far north as the Dakotas. In the meantime, a new menace had appeared in the form of the advancing frontier of population. The construction of the Santa Fe Railway through Dodge City, Kan., to La Junta, Colo., permitted cattlemen to move their operations westward ahead of the settlers; Dodge City replaced Abilene as the principal centre for the annual meeting of cattlemen and buyers.

Despite sporadic conflicts with settlers encroaching upon the high plains, the open range survived until a series of savage blizzards struck the plains with unprecedented fury in the winter of 1886–87, killing hundreds of thousands of cattle and forcing many owners into bankruptcy. Those who still had some cattle and some capital abandoned the open range, gained title to lands farther west, where they could provide shelter for their livestock, and revived a cattle industry on land that would be immune to further advances of the frontier of settlement. Their removal to these new lands had been made possible in part by the construction of other railroads connecting the region with Chicago and the Pacific coast.

THE EXPANSION OF THE RAILROADS

In 1862 Congress authorized the construction of two railroads that together would provide the first railroad link between the Mississippi valley and the

Railroad officials and workers celebrating the driving of the Golden Spike, marking the completion of the transcontinental railroad at Promontory Summit, Utah Territory, 1869. MPI/Archive Photos/Getty Images

Pacific coast. One was the Union Pacific, to run westward from Council Bluffs, Iowa, and the other was the Central Pacific, to run eastward from Sacramento, Calif. To encourage the rapid completion of those roads, Congress provided generous subsidies in the form of land grants and loans. Construction was slower than Congress had anticipated, but the two lines met, with elaborate ceremonies, on May 10, 1869, at Promontory, Utah.

In the meantime, other railroads had begun construction westward, but the panic of 1873 and the ensuing depression halted or delayed progress on many of those lines. With the return of prosperity after 1877, some railroads resumed or accelerated construction. By 1883 three more rail connections between the Mississippi valley and the West Coast had been completed: the Northern Pacific, from St. Paul to Portland; the Santa Fe, from Chicago to Los Angeles; and the Southern Pacific, from New Orleans to Los Angeles. The Southern Pacific also had acquired, by purchase or construction, lines from Portland to San Francisco and from San Francisco to Los Angeles.

The construction of the railroads from the Midwest to the Pacific coast was the railroad builders' most spectacular achievement in the quarter century after the Civil War. No less important, in terms of the national economy, was the development in the same period of an adequate rail network in the Southern states and the building of other railroads that connected virtually every important community west of the Mississippi with Chicago.

The West developed simultaneously with the building of the Western railroads, and in no part of the country was the importance of railroads more generally recognized. The railroad gave vitality to the regions it served, but, by withholding service, it could doom a community to stagnation. The railroads appeared to be ruthless in exploiting their powerful position. They fixed prices to suit their convenience, discriminated among their customers, and attempted to gain a monopoly of transportation wherever possible. They also interfered in state and local politics to elect favourites to office, block unfriendly legislation, and even influence the decisions of the courts.

INDIAN POLICY

Large tracts of land in the West were reserved by law for the exclusive use of specified Indian tribes. By 1870, however, the invasion of these lands by hordes of prospectors, cattlemen and farmers, and the transcontinental railroads had resulted in the outbreak of a series of savage Indian wars, and had raised serious questions about the government's Indian policies. Many agents of the Bureau of Indian Affairs were lax in their responsibility for dealing directly with the tribes, and some were corrupt in the discharge of their duties. Most Westerners and some army officers contended that the only satisfactory resolution of the Indian question was the removal of the tribes from all lands coveted by the whites.

Document: Chief Joseph: The Disillusioned Indian (1879)

The discovery of gold on the reservation of the Nez Percé Indians in the Oregon country led to an overrunning of their land by miners in 1860. By coercion and bribery the government traduced some of the chiefs into signing away their land in a treaty three years later. Many of the Nez Percé remained, and when, in 1877, the government attempted to force them to leave, the tribe reacted, and under the leadership of Chief Joseph fought the U.S. Army for four months before being subdued in northern Montana.

The Nez Percé were sent to the barren lands of the Oklahoma Indian Territory, where many of them fell victim to malaria and other diseases. Chief Joseph continued to plead the cause of his people, and eventually the remainder of the nation was allowed to return to the Northwest. In 1879 an account by Chief Joseph described the events leading up to the conflict of 1877 and its aftermath. The melancholy closing portion of his narrative is reprinted here.

During the hot days [July 1878] we received notice that we were to be moved farther away from our own country. We were not asked if we were willing to go. We were ordered to get into the railroad cars. Three of my people died on the way to Baxter Springs. It was worse to die there than to die fighting in the mountains.

We were moved from Baxter Springs [Kansas] to the Indian Territory, and set down without our lodges. We had but little medicine, and we were nearly all sick. Seventy of my people have died since we moved there.

We have had a great many visitors who have talked many ways. Some of the chiefs [General Fish and Colonel Stickney] from Washington came to see us, and selected land for us to live upon. We have not moved to that land, for it is not a good place to live.

The commissioner chief [E. A. Hayt] came to see us. I told him, as I told every one, that I expected General Miles's word would be carried out. He said it "could not be done; that white men now lived in my country and all the land was taken up; that, if I returned to Wallowa, I could not live in peace; that law-papers were out against my young men who began the war, and that the government could not protect my people." This talk fell like a heavy stone upon my heart. I saw that I could not gain anything by talking to him. Other law chiefs [congressional committee] came to see me and said they would help me to get a healthy country. I did not know who to believe. The white people have too many chiefs. They do not understand each other. They do not all talk alike....

In the immediate postwar years, reformers advocated adoption of programs designed to prepare the Indians for ultimate assimilation into American society. In 1869 the reformers persuaded Pres. Ulysses S. Grant and Congress to establish a nonpolitical Board of Indian Commissioners to supervise the administration of relations between the government and the Indians. The board, however, encountered so much political opposition that it accomplished little. The reformers then proposed legislation to grant title for specific acreages of land

Horses grazing along the perimeter of Native American encampment in Montana Territory 1887. That year Congress enacted the Dawes Act, which granted land to Indians willing to be assimilated. George Eastman House/Archive Photos/Getty Images

to the head of each family in those tribes thought to be ready to adopt a sedentary life as farmers. Congress resisted that proposal until land-hungry Westerners discovered that if the land were thus distributed, a vast surplus of land would result that could be added to the public domain. When land speculators joined the reformers in support of the proposed legislation, Congress, in 1887, enacted the Dawes Act, which empowered the president to grant title to 160 acres (65 hectares) to the head of each family, with smaller allotments to single members of the tribe, in those tribes believed ready

to accept a new way of life as farmers. With the grant of land, which could not be alienated by the Indians for 25 years, they were to be granted U.S. citizenship.

Reformers rejoiced that they had finally given the Indians an opportunity to have a dignified role in U.S. society, overlooking the possibility that there might be values in Indian culture worthy of preservation. Meanwhile, the land promoters placed successive presidents under great pressure to accelerate the application of the Dawes Act in order to open more land for occupation or speculation.

CHAPTER 3

THE GROWTH OF INDUSTRY

By 1878 the United States had reentered a period of prosperity after the long depression of the mid-1870s. In the ensuing 20 years the volume of industrial production, the number of workers employed in industry, and the number of manufacturing plants all more than doubled. A more accurate index to the scope of this industrial advance may be found in the aggregate annual value of all manufactured goods, which increased from about $5.4 billion in 1879 to perhaps $13 billion in 1899. The expansion of the iron and steel industry, always a key factor in any industrial economy, was even more impressive. From 1880 to 1900, the annual production of steel in the United States went from about 1.4 million to more than 11 million tons. Before the end of the century, the United States surpassed Great Britain in the production of iron and steel and was providing more than one-quarter of the world's supply of pig iron.

Many factors combined to produce this burst of industrial activity. The exploitation of Western resources, including mines and lumber, stimulated a demand for improved transportation, while the gold and silver mines provided new sources of capital for investment in the East.

Illustration of men working in a Pittsburgh, Pa., steel mill in the 1880s. In the last two decades of the 19th century, production of steel rose sharply in the United States. PhotoQuest/Archive Photos/Getty Images

The demand for steel rails that accompanied the construction of railroads, especially in the West and South, was a major force in the expansion of the steel industry; railroad mileage in the United States went from less than 93,262 miles (150,151 kilometres) in 1880 to about 190,000 miles (310,000 kilometres) in 1900. Technological advances, including the utilization of the Bessemer and open-hearth processes in the manufacture of steel, resulted in improved products and lower production costs. A series of major inventions, including the telephone, typewriter, linotype, phonograph, electric light, cash register, air brake, refrigerator car, and the automobile, became the bases for new industries, while many of them revolutionized the conduct of business. The use of petroleum products in industry, as well as for domestic heating and lighting, became the cornerstone of the most powerful of the new industries of the period, while the trolley car, the increased use of gas and electric power, and the telephone led to the establishment of important public utilities that were natural monopolies and could operate only on the basis of franchises granted by state or municipal governments. The widespread employment of the corporate form of business organization offered new opportunities for large-scale financing of business enterprise and attracted new capital, much of it furnished by European investors.

Document: Andrew Carnegie: The Picture Lover and Picture Buyer (1886)

Although steel manufacturer Andrew Carnegie managed to make money at a nearly unprecedented rate, he always maintained that his real interests and goals in life were other than monetary—were instead learning, writing, the arts, and public benevolence. He frequently contributed articles on a variety of subjects to journals such as the North American Review, *and in 1886 he published a book,* Triumphant Democracy, *in which he set out to demonstrate the superiority of American institutions to those of the Old World, especially Britain. The following selection from that work is taken from the chapter entitled "Art—Painting and Sculpture."*

Art, in fact, is the effort of man to express the ideas which nature suggests to him of a power above nature, whether that power be within the recesses of his own being, or in the Great First Cause of which nature, like himself, is but the effect. —Bulwer.

If side by side with progress in material things there was not found corresponding progress in the higher things of the spirit, there would be but little cause for congratulation among the citizens of the republic. If there was not spreading among the masses of the people along with their material blessings a love of the beautiful; if with their comforts there did not come the love of music; if, in short, "art," using the term in its broadest sense, did not shed everywhere around its elevating influence, we should have little reason to be proud or hopeful of our country, much less to extol it. To reach her proper position and play her part among the nations, she must not only be the wealthiest country in the world but richest in the diffusion of refinement and culture among the people....

Over all this industrial activity there presided a colourful and energetic group of entrepreneurs who gained the attention, if not always the commendation, of the public and who appeared to symbolize for the public the new class of leadership in the United States. Of this numerous group the best known were John D. Rockefeller in oil, Andrew Carnegie in steel, and such railroad builders and promoters as Cornelius Vanderbilt, Leland Stanford, Collis P. Huntington, Henry Villard, and James J. Hill.

THE DISPERSION OF INDUSTRY

The period was notable also for the wide geographic distribution of industry. The Eastern Seaboard from Massachusetts to Pennsylvania continued to be the most heavily industrialized section of the United States, but there was substantial development of manufacturing in the states adjacent to the Great Lakes and certain sections of the South.

Lustige Blätter.]
Andrew Carnegie.
Steel King.

Pierpont Morgan.
Trust King.

William Rockefeller.
Oil King.

A cartoon depicting (left to right) *Andrew Carnegie, J.P. Morgan, and William Rockefeller (brother of John D. Rockefeller) as kings of American industry.* Hulton Archive/Getty Images

The experience of the steel industry reflected this new pattern of diffusion. Two-thirds of the iron and steel industry was concentrated in the area of western Pennsylvania and eastern Ohio. After 1880, however, the development of iron mines in northern Minnesota (the Vermilion Range in 1884 and the Mesabi Range in 1892), as well as Tennessee and northern Alabama, was followed by the expansion of the iron and steel industry in the Chicago area and the establishment of steel mills in northern Alabama and Tennessee.

Most manufacturing in the Midwest was in enterprises closely associated with agriculture and represented expansion of industries that had first been established before 1860. Meat-packing, which in the years after 1875 became one of the major industries of the country in terms of the value of its products, was almost a Midwestern monopoly, with a large part of the industry concentrated in Chicago. Flour milling, brewing, and the manufacture of farm machinery and lumber products were other important Midwestern industries.

The industrial invasion of the South was spearheaded by textiles. Cotton mills became the symbol of the New South, and mills and mill towns sprang up in the Piedmont region from Virginia to Georgia and into Alabama. By 1900 almost one-quarter of all the cotton spindles in the United States were in the South, and Southern mills were expanding their operations more rapidly than were their well-established competitors in New England. The development of lumbering in the South was even more impressive, though less publicized; by the end of the century the South led the country in lumber production, contributing almost one-third of the annual supply.

INDUSTRIAL COMBINATIONS

The geographic dispersal of industry was part of a movement that was converting the United States into an industrial country. It attracted less attention, however, than the trend toward the consolidation of competing firms into large units capable of dominating an entire industry. The movement toward consolidation received special attention in 1882 when Rockefeller and his associates organized the Standard Oil Trust under the laws of Ohio. A trust was a new type of industrial organization, in which the voting rights of a controlling number of shares of competing firms were entrusted to a small group of men, or trustees, who thus were able to prevent competition among the companies they controlled. The stockholders presumably benefited through the larger dividends they received. For a few years the trust was a popular vehicle for the creation of monopolies, and by 1890 there were trusts in whiskey, lead, cottonseed oil, and salt.

In 1892 the courts of Ohio ruled that the trust violated that state's anti-monopoly laws. Standard Oil then reincorporated as a holding company

The spinning room of the White Oak Cotton Mill in Greensboro, N.C. Textiles were a burgeoning industry in the South following the Civil War. Archive Photos/Getty Images

under the more hospitable laws of New Jersey. Thereafter, holding companies or outright mergers became the favourite forms for the creation of monopolies, though the term *trust* remained in the popular vocabulary as a common description of any monopoly. The best-known mergers of the period were those leading to the formation of the American Tobacco Company (1890) and the American Sugar Refining Company (1891). The latter was especially successful in stifling competition, for it quickly gained control of most of the sugar refined in the United States.

FOREIGN COMMERCE

The foreign trade of the United States, if judged by the value of exports, kept pace with the growth of domestic industry. Exclusive of gold, silver, and re-exports, the annual value of exports from the United States in 1877 was about $590 million; by 1900 it had increased to nearly $1.4 billion. The value of imports also rose, though at a slower rate. When gold and silver are included, there was only one year in the entire period in which the United States had an unfavourable

Document: Henry Demarest Lloyd: Monopoly and Social Control (1884)

Henry Demarest Lloyd, the earliest of the social reformers who were later to be called "muckrakers," became familiar with the problem of trusts and monopolies while financial editor of the Chicago Tribune. *His "Story of a Great Monopoly" (1881) exposed the methods of the Standard Oil and railroad trusts and established him as a champion of the consumer, the independent competitor, and the labourer. Lloyd's conviction that "liberty and monopoly cannot live together" and that goods "cooperatively produced [must be] cooperatively enjoyed" led him to attack all forms of monopoly in "Lords of Industry," an article published in the* North American Review, *portions of which follow.*

When President Gowen of the Reading Railroad was defending that company, in 1875, before a committee of the Pennsylvania legislature, for having taken part in the combination of the coal companies to cure the evil of "too much coal" by putting up the price and cutting down the amount for sale, he pleaded that there were fifty trades in which the same thing was done. He had a list of them to show the committee. He said:

> Every pound of rope we buy for our vessels or for our mines is bought at a price fixed by a committee of the rope manufacturers of the United States. Every keg of nails, every paper of tacks, all our screws and wrenches and hinges, the boiler flues for our locomotives are never bought except at the price fixed by the representatives of the mills that manufacture them. Iron beams for your houses or your bridges can be had

only at the prices agreed upon by a combination of those who produce them. Fire brick, gas pipe, terra-cotta pipe for drainage, every keg of powder we buy to blast coal are purchased under the same arrangement. Every pane of window glass in this house was bought at a scale of prices established exactly in the same manner. White lead, galvanized sheet iron, hose and belting and files are bought and sold at a rate determined in the same way....

balance of trade, and as the century drew to a close, the excess of exports over imports increased perceptibly.

Agriculture continued to furnish the bulk of U.S. exports. Cotton, wheat, flour, and meat products were consistently the items with the greatest annual value among exports. Of the nonagricultural products sent abroad, petroleum was the most important, though by the end of the century its position on the list of exports was being challenged by machinery.

Despite the expansion of foreign trade, the U.S. merchant marine was a major casualty of the period. While the aggregate tonnage of all shipping flying the U.S. flag remained remarkably constant, the tonnage engaged in foreign trade declined sharply, dropping from more than 2.4 million tons on the eve of the Civil War to a low point of only 726,000 tons in 1898. The decline began during the Civil War when hundreds of ships were transferred to foreign registries to avoid destruction. Later, cost disadvantages in shipbuilding and repair, along with the American policy of registering only American-built ships, hindered growth until World War I.

CHAPTER 4

LABOUR

The expansion of industry was accompanied by increased tensions between employers and workers. Also entering the mix was the appearance, for the first time in the United States, of national labour unions.

FORMATION OF UNIONS

The first effective labour organization that was more than regional in membership and influence was the Knights of Labor, organized in 1869. The Knights believed in the unity of the interests of all producing groups and sought to enlist in their ranks not only all labourers but everyone who could be truly classified as a producer. They championed a variety of causes, many of them more political than industrial, and they hoped to gain their ends through politics and education rather than through economic coercion.

The hardships suffered by many workers during the depression of 1873–78 and the failure of a nationwide railroad strike, which was broken when Pres. Rutherford B. Hayes sent federal troops to suppress disorders in Pittsburgh

Women delegates to the 1886 Knights of Labor Convention. Knights' membership included African Americans and women, reflecting the organization's support of equality in the workplace. Fotosearch/Archive Photos/Getty Images

Document: The Knights of Labor (1878)

The traditional premium placed upon craftsmanship in handwork was rapidly supplanted during the Industrial Revolution by new demands for efficiency in mass production. Skilled workmen such as shoemakers, machinists, molders, coopers, garment workers, and cigar makers seemed most likely to be replaced by machines and were most amenable to the protection offered by trade unions. The Noble Order of the Knights of Labor, founded in 1869 by Uriah Stephens, enlisted the garment workers of Philadelphia into a common cause under the motto, "An injury to one is the concern of all." The Constitution of the Knights of Labor was written in 1874; the Preamble, reprinted below, drafted by Terence V. Powderly and Robert Schilling, was adopted Jan. 3, 1878.

The recent alarming development and aggression of aggregated wealth, which, unless checked, will invariably lead to the pauperization and hopeless degradation of the toiling masses, render it imperative, if we desire to enjoy the blessings of life, that a check should be placed upon its power and upon unjust accumulation, and a system adopted which will secure to the laborer the fruits of his toil. And as this much-desired object can only be accomplished by the thorough unification of labor and the united efforts of those who obey the divine injunction that "In the sweat of thy brow shalt thou eat bread," we have formed the ——— with a view of securing the organization and direction, by cooperative effort, of the power of the industrial classes; and we submit to the world the objects sought to be accomplished by our organization, calling upon all who believe in securing "the greatest good to the greatest number" to aid and assist us:

- To bring within the folds of organization every department of productive industry, making knowledge a standpoint for action and industrial and moral worth, not wealth, the true standard of individual and national greatness.
- To secure to the toilers a proper share of the wealth that they create; more of the leisure that rightfully belongs to them; more societary advantages; more of the benefits, privileges, and emoluments of the world; in a word, all those rights and privileges necessary to make them capable of enjoying, appreciating, defending, and perpetuating the blessings of good government....

and St. Louis, caused much discontent in the ranks of the Knights. In 1879 Terence V. Powderly, a railroad worker and mayor of Scranton, Pa., was elected grand master workman of the national organization. He favoured cooperation over a program of aggressive action, but the effective control of the Knights shifted to regional leaders who were willing to initiate strikes or other forms of economic pressure to gain their objectives. The Knights reached the peak of their influence in 1884–85, when much-publicized strikes against the Union Pacific, Southwest System, and Wabash railroads attracted substantial public sympathy and succeeded in preventing a reduction in wages. At that time they claimed a national membership of nearly 700,000. In 1885 Congress, taking note of the apparently increasing power of labour, acceded to union demands to prohibit the entry into the United States of immigrants who had signed contracts to work for specific employers.

The year 1886 was a troubled one in labour relations. There were nearly 1,600 strikes, involving about 600,000 workers, with the eight-hour day the most prominent item in the demands of labour. About half of these strikes were called for May Day (May 1). Some of them were successful, but the failure of others and internal conflicts between skilled and unskilled members led to a decline in the Knights' popularity and influence.

THE HAYMARKET RIOT

The most serious blow to the unions came from a tragic occurrence with which they were only indirectly associated. One of the strikes called for May Day in 1886 was against the McCormick Harvesting Machine Company in Chicago. Fighting broke out along the picket lines on May 3. When police intervened to restore order, several strikers were injured or killed. Union leaders called a protest meeting at Haymarket Square for the evening of May 4, but as the meeting was breaking up, a group of anarchists took over and began to make inflammatory speeches. The police quickly intervened, and then a bomb exploded, killing seven policemen and injuring many others. Eight of the anarchists were arrested, tried, and convicted of murder. Four of them were hanged and one committed suicide. The remaining three were pardoned in 1893 by Gov. John P. Altgeld, who was persuaded that they had been convicted in such an atmosphere of prejudice that it was impossible to be certain that they were guilty.

Colourized engraving of a scene from the Haymarket Riot. Support for unions declined after the incident, in which seven police officers were killed. Stock Montage/Archive Photos/Getty Images

Document: The Pullman Strike and Boycott (1894)

George Pullman's Palace Car Company and "model" community near Chicago were severely affected by the depression following the Panic of 1893. In response to the decreasing demand for railroad cars, the Pullman Company reduced its work force, shortened the workweek, and decreased wages by 25 percent but refused to lower rents in the company-owned community of Pullman.

Early in 1894 large numbers of Pullman employees joined the American Railway Union (ARU), which called a meeting with company officials on May 9, at which the employees requested that wages be restored to the levels of the previous year. The company refused on the grounds that lowered business volume would not support such wages. The following day—contrary to a promise exacted in the meeting—three members of the employees' committee were fired. The local union immediately called a strike. The company refused to negotiate with the ARU, and the union thereupon ordered a nationwide boycott of Pullman cars on June 26.

The struggle between the General Managers' Association, which discharged switchmen who refused to handle Pullman cars, and the ARU, which struck again after each dismissal, spread until virtually all of the railroads came to a standstill. The issues that crystallized in the dispute are still under debate. The statement from the Pullman strikers was addressed to the Convention of the ARU, assembled in Chicago, June 15, 1894; the Pullman Company's statement in defense of its action first appeared in the Chicago Herald, *June 26, 1894.*

I. Statement of the Strikers

Mr. President and brothers of the American Railway Union: We struck at Pullman because we were without hope. We joined the American Railway Union because it gave us a glimmer of hope. Twenty thousand souls, men, women, and little ones, have their eyes turned toward this convention today, straining eagerly through dark despondency for a glimmer of the heaven-sent message you alone can give us on this earth.

In stating to this body our grievances, it is hard to tell where to begin. You all must know that the proximate cause of our strike was the discharge of two members of our Grievance Committee the day after George M. Pullman, himself, and Thomas H. Wickes, his second vice-president, had guaranteed them absolute immunity. The more remote causes are still imminent. Five reductions in wages, in work, and in conditions of employment swept through the shops at Pullman between May and December 1893. The last was the most severe, amounting to nearly 30 percent, and our rents had not fallen. We owed Pullman $70,000 when we struck May 11. We owe him twice as much today. He does not evict us for two reasons: one, the force of popular sentiment and public opinion; the other, because he hopes to starve us out, to break through in the back of the American Railway Union, and to deduct from our miserable wages when we are forced to return to him the last dollar we owe him for the occupancy of his houses....

The public tended to blame organized labour for the Haymarket tragedy, and many people had become convinced that the activities of unions were likely to be attended by violence. The Knights never regained the ground they lost in 1886, and, until after the turn of the century, organized labour seldom gained any measure of public sympathy. Aggregate union membership did not again reach its 1885–86 figure until 1900. Unions, however, continued to be active; in each year from 1889 through the end of the century there were more than 1,000 strikes.

As the power of the Knights declined, the leadership in the trade union movement passed to the American Federation of Labor (AFL). This was a loose federation of local and craft unions, organized first in 1881 and reorganized in 1886. For a few years there was some nominal cooperation between the Knights and the AFL, but the basic organization and philosophy of the two groups made

Document: Samuel Gompers: The Laborer's Light to Life (1894)

A popular tool for curbing union effectiveness in the 1890s was the court injunction prohibiting union members from engaging in strike activities. Such an injunction was issued in the 1894 Pullman strike by the U.S. District Court of Illinois, impairing the strength of the American Railway Union in that struggle. Eugene V. Debs, president of the ARU, was summoned before a grand jury for violating the injunction. In his charge to the jury, Judge Peter

Samuel Gompers, first president of the American Federation of Labor. Library of Congress, Washington, D.C

Grosscup made use of the traditional anti-union argument that union organizing constituted a conspiracy.

Samuel Gompers, president of the American Federation of Labor, was asked by the North American Review *to write an article about the strike, which elicited a letter from Grosscup pointing out that Gompers had misquoted him. Gompers's reply to Grosscup on Aug. 14, 1894, reprinted here, continued his attack on the judge's charge to the jury.*

Dear Sir:

I have the honor to acknowledge the receipt of your favor of the 31st ult., the contents of which I have carefully noted. Possibly I should have written you earlier, but more important matters demanded my immediate consideration. I hope, however, that you have suffered no inconvenience or pain of injustice done you by reason of this delay.

You say that I have misquoted you in my article in the *North American Review* in attributing to you the following words in your Decoration Day address at Galesburg: "The growth of labor organizations must be restrained by law." Upon closer examination you will find that I did not use the word "restrained," but "checked." However, this makes little material difference, except to show that unintentionally one man may misquote another.

The words I quoted I saw in several newspaper accounts of your address, and I am exceedingly pleased that you favor me with a printed copy of it, which I have read with much interest. In perusing that address I find that you said (page 12): "Restore to each individual by the enforcement of law, not simply his right but if possible a returning sense of duty to control his own personality and property. Let us set a limit to the field of organization."...

cooperation difficult. The AFL appealed only to skilled workers, and its objectives were those of immediate concern to its members: hours, wages, working conditions, and the recognition of the union. It relied on economic weapons, chiefly the strike and boycott, and it eschewed political activity, except for state and local election campaigns. The central figure in the AFL was Samuel Gompers, a New York cigar maker who was the group's president from 1886 to his death in 1924.

CHAPTER 5

NATIONAL POLITICS

The dominant forces in American life in the last quarter of the 19th century were economic and social rather than political. This fact was reflected in the ineffectiveness of political leadership and in the absence of deeply divisive issues in politics, except perhaps for the continuing agrarian agitation for inflation. There were colourful political personalities, but they gained their following on a personal basis rather than as spokesmen for a program of political action. No president of the period was truly the leader of his party, and none apparently aspired to that status except Grover Cleveland during his second term (1893–97). Such shrewd observers of U.S. politics as Woodrow Wilson and James Bryce agreed that great men did not become presidents; and it was clear that the nominating conventions of both major parties commonly selected candidates who were "available" in the sense that they had few enemies.

Congress had been steadily increasing in power since the administration of Andrew Johnson and, in the absence of leadership from the White House, was largely responsible for formulating public policy. As a result, public policy commonly represented a compromise among the views of many

Document: Woodrow Wilson:
The Declining Prestige of the Presidential Office (1885)

A series of weak presidents in the 10 years or so before the Civil War opened the way for the U.S. Senate to assume a dominant position in the federal government. The towering figure of Abraham Lincoln reversed the trend, but the postwar controversies between the executive and the legislative branches over Reconstruction resulted in the reassertion of congressional dominance.

Future president Woodrow Wilson analyzed this rift between the executive and legislative branches of government in his first book, Congressional Government. *The book, which was his doctoral thesis at Johns Hopkins University, was published in 1885. The following selection is from the introduction.*

We are the first Americans to hear our own countrymen ask whether the Constitution is still adapted to serve the purposes for which it was intended; the first to entertain any serious doubts about the superiority of our own institutions as compared with the systems of Europe; the first to think of remodeling the administrative machinery of the federal government and of forcing new forms of responsibility upon Congress.

The evident explanation of this change of attitude toward the Constitution is that we have been made conscious, by the rude shock of the war and by subsequent developments of policy, that there has been a vast alteration in the conditions of government; that the checks and balances which once obtained are no longer effective; and that we are really living under a Constitution essentially different from that which we have been so long worshiping as our own peculiar and incomparable possession. In short, this model government is no longer conformable with its own original pattern. While we have been shielding it from criticism it has slipped away from us....

Pres. Woodrow Wilson, throwing out the first ball on opening day of the Major League baseball season, 1916. Library of Congress Prints and Photographs Division

congressional leaders—a situation made more essential because of the fact that in only four of the 20 years from 1877 to 1897 did the same party control the White House, the Senate, and the House.

The Republicans appeared to be the majority party in national politics. From the Civil War to the end of the century, they won every presidential election save those of 1884 and 1892, and they had a majority in the Senate in all but three Congresses during that same period. The Democrats, however, won a majority in the House in eight of the 10 Congresses from 1875 to 1895. The success of the Republicans was achieved in the face of bitter intraparty schisms that plagued Republican leaders from 1870 until after 1890 and despite the fact that, in every election campaign after 1876, they were forced to concede the entire South to the opposition. The

Poster of the winning ticket in the 1884 U.S. presidential election, Grover Cleveland and Thomas A. Hendricks. Cleveland was the only Democrat to serve as president (1884, 1892) between 1869 and 1900. Buyenlarge/Archive Photos/Getty Images

The Gilded Age

The 1870s in the United States were a period of gross materialism and blatant political corruption that gave rise to important novels of social and political criticism. The period takes its name from the earliest of these, The Gilded Age *(1873), written by Mark Twain in collaboration with Charles Dudley Warner. The novel gives a vivid and accurate description of Washington, D.C., and is peopled with caricatures of many leading figures of the day, including greedy industrialists and corrupt politicians.*

Twain's satire was followed in 1880 by Democracy, *a political novel published anonymously by the historian Henry Adams. Adams's book deals with a dishonest Midwestern senator and suggests that the real source of corruption lies in the unprincipled attitudes of the wild and lawless West.* An American Politician, *by Francis Marion Crawford (1884), focussed upon the disputed election of Pres. Rutherford B. Hayes in 1876, but its significance as a political novel is diluted by an overdose of popular romance.*

The political novels of the Gilded Age represent the beginnings of a new strain in American literature, the novel as a vehicle of social protest. This was a trend that grew in the late 19th and early 20th centuries with the works of the muckrakers and culminated in those of the proletarian novelists.

Republicans had the advantage of having been the party that had defended the Union against secession and had freed the slaves. When all other appeals failed, Republican leaders could salvage votes in the North and West by reviving memories of the war.

A less tangible but equally valuable advantage was the widespread belief that the continued industrial development of the country would be more secure under a Republican than a Democratic administration. Except in years of economic adversity, the memory of the war and confidence in the economic program of the Republican Party were normally enough to ensure Republican success in most of the Northern and Western states.

CHAPTER 6

THE RUTHERFORD B. HAYES ADMINISTRATION

President Hayes (served 1877–81) willingly carried out the commitments made by his friends to secure the disputed Southern votes needed for his election. He withdrew the federal troops still in the South, and he appointed former senator David M. Key of Tennessee to his cabinet as postmaster general. Hayes hoped that these conciliatory gestures would encourage many Southern conservatives to support the Republican Party in the future. But the Southerners' primary concern was the maintenance of white supremacy; this, they believed, required a monopoly of political power in the South by the Democratic Party. As a result, the policies of Hayes led to the virtual extinction rather than the revival of the Republican Party in the South.

Hayes's efforts to woo the South irritated some Republicans, but his attitude toward patronage in the federal civil service was a more immediate challenge to his party. In June 1877 he issued an executive order prohibiting political activity by those who held federal appointments. When two friends of Sen. Roscoe Conkling defied this order, Hayes removed them from their posts in the administration of the Port of New York. Conkling and his associates showed their contempt for Hayes by bringing about the election of one of the men (Alonzo B. Cornell) as governor of New York in 1879 and by nominating the other (Chester A. Arthur) as

Document: Rutherford B. Hayes: Wealth in the Hands of the Few (1886–87)

Unlike most of his fellow Republicans, President Hayes held an unsympathetic attitude toward the trusts. This was one of many issues that caused Hayes to lose the support of portions of the party early in his administration. Having left the White House in 1881 after only one term, Hayes retired to his Ohio home and occupied himself with enlarging his library, fulfilling numerous speaking engagements, and working for humanitarian causes. His concern over the power of concentrated wealth is illustrated by the following passages from his diary, written in 1886 and 1887.

January 22, 1886. Friday. How to distribute more equally the property of our country is a question we (Theodore Clapp and I) considered yesterday. We ought not to allow a permanent aristocracy of inherited wealth to grow up in our country. How would it answer to limit the amount that

Rutherford B. Hayes. Library of Congress (neg. no. LC-USZ62-13019)

could be left to any one person by will or otherwise? What should be the limit? Let no one receive from another more than the law gives to the chief justice, to the general of the Army, or to the president of the Senate. Let the income of the property transmitted equal this, say $10,000 to $20,000. If after distributing on this principle there remains undistributed part of the estate, let it go to the public. The object is to secure a distribution of great estates to prevent accumulation.

January 24. Sunday. The question for the country now is how to secure a more equal distribution of property among the people. There can be no republican institutions with vast masses of property permanently in a few hands, and large masses of voters without property. To begin the work, as a first step, prevent large estates from passing, by wills or by inheritance or by corporations, into the hands of a single man. Let no man get by inheritance or by will more than will produce at 4 percent interest an income equal to the salary paid to the chief justice, to the general of the Army, or to the highest officer of the Navy — say an income of $15,000 per year or an estate of $500,000....

Republican candidate for the vice presidency in 1880.

One of the most serious issues facing Hayes was that of inflation. Hayes and many other Republicans were staunch supporters of a sound-money policy, but the issues were sectional rather than partisan. In general, sentiment in the agricultural South and West was favourable to inflation, while industrial and financial groups in the Northeast opposed any move to inflate the currency, holding that this would benefit debtors at the expense of creditors.

In 1873 Congress had discontinued the minting of silver dollars, an action later stigmatized by friends of silver as the Crime of '73. As the depression deepened, inflationists began campaigns to persuade Congress to resume coinage of silver dollars and repeal the act providing for the redemption of Civil War greenbacks in gold after Jan. 1, 1879. By 1878 the sentiment for silver and inflation was so strong that Congress passed, over the president's veto, the Bland–Allison Act, which renewed the coinage of silver dollars and, more significantly, included a mandate to the secretary of the treasury to purchase silver bullion at the market price in amounts of not less than $2 million and not more than $4 million each month.

Opponents of inflation were somewhat reassured by the care with which Secretary of the Treasury John Sherman was making preparation to have an adequate gold reserve to meet any demands on the Treasury for the redemption of greenbacks. Equally reassuring were indications that the country had at last recovered from the long period of depression. These factors reestablished confidence in the financial stability of the government; when the date for the redemption of greenbacks arrived, there was no appreciable demand upon the Treasury to exchange them for gold.

Hayes chose not to run for reelection. Had he sought a second term, he would almost certainly have been denied renomination by the Republican leaders, many of whom he had alienated through his policies of patronage reform and Southern conciliation. Three prominent candidates contended for the Republican nomination in 1880: Grant, the choice of the "Stalwart" faction led by Senator Conkling; James G. Blaine, the leader of the rival "Half-Breed" faction; and Secretary of the Treasury Sherman. Grant had a substantial and loyal bloc of delegates in the convention, but their number was short of a majority. Neither of the other candidates could command a majority, and on the 36th ballot the weary delegates nominated a compromise candidate, Congressman James A. Garfield of Ohio. To placate the Stalwart faction, the convention nominated Chester A. Arthur of New York for vice president.

The Democrats probably would have renominated Samuel J. Tilden in 1880, hoping thereby to gain votes from those who believed Tilden had lost in 1876 through fraud. But Tilden declined

John Sherman, who was secretary of the treasury under Pres. Rutherford B. Hayes. Sherman also vied for the Republican presidential nomination in 1880, 1884, and 1888. Library of Congress Prints and Photographs Division

Civil War Union general and Democratic presidential nominee Winfield S. Hancock. Bob Thomas/Popperfoto/Getty Images

growth of domestic industry. Actually, the Democrats were badly divided on the tariff, and Hancock surprised political leaders of both parties by declaring that the tariff was an issue of only local interest.

Garfield won the election with an electoral margin of 214 to 155, but his plurality in the popular vote was a slim 9,644. The election revealed the existence of a new "solid South," for Hancock carried all the former Confederate states and three of the former slave states that had remained loyal to the Union.

to become a candidate again, and the Democratic convention nominated Gen. Winfield S. Hancock, who had been a Federal general during the Civil War. Hancock had no political record and little familiarity with questions of public policy.

The campaign failed to generate any unusual excitement and produced no novel issues. As in every national election of the period, the Republicans stressed their role as the party of the protective tariff and asserted that Democratic opposition to the tariff would impede the

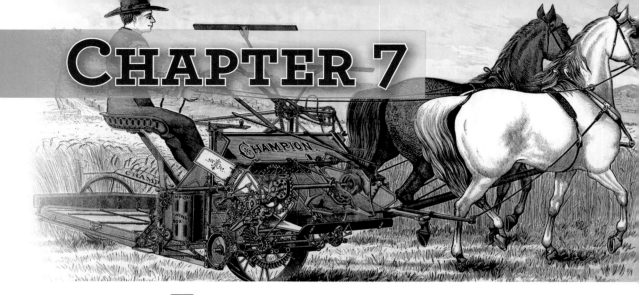

CHAPTER 7

THE ADMINISTRATIONS OF JAMES A. GARFIELD AND CHESTER A. ARTHUR

Garfield had not been closely identified with either the Stalwarts or the Half-Breeds, the two major factions within the Republican Party, but, upon becoming president, he upset the Stalwarts by naming the Half-Breed James G. Blaine secretary of state. He gave even more serious offense to the Stalwart faction by appointing as collector of customs at New York a man who was unacceptable to the two senators from that state, Roscoe Conkling and Thomas Platt, who showed their displeasure by resigning their Senate seats, expecting to be reelected triumphantly by the legislature of New York; in this they were disappointed.

The tragic climax to this intraparty strife came on July 2, 1881, when Garfield was shot in Washington, D.C., by a disappointed and mentally deranged office seeker and Stalwart supporter named Charles Guiteau. For two months the president lingered between life and death. He died on September 19 and was succeeded by Vice President Arthur.

Artist's rendition of the assassination of Pres. James Garfield. Three Lions/Hulton Archive/ Getty Images

Document: "Charles Guiteau" (1882)

Pres. James A. Garfield had been in office for only four months when he was shot (July 2, 1881) by Charles J. Guiteau, a failed lawyer, preacher, and would-be politician, who claimed to be a member of the Stalwart wing of the Republican Party. Garfield died Sept. 19, 1881. The following song shows Guiteau lamenting his trial and coming execution. Guiteau, who unsuccessfully pleaded insanity at his trial and elected to defend himself in court, was executed on June 30, 1882.

CHARLES GUITEAU

Come all you Christian people, wherever you may be,
And please pay close attention to these few lines from me.
On the thirtieth day of June, I am condemned to die
For the murder of James A. Garfield, upon the scaffold high.

Chorus:

My name is Charles Guiteau, my name I'll never deny,
To leave my aged parents in sorrow for to die,
But little did I think, while in my youthful bloom,
I'd be carried to the scaffold to meet my fatal doom.
I tried to play off insane, but found it would not do,
The people all against me, it proved to make no show.
Judge Cox he passed the sentence, and the clerk he wrote it down,
On the thirtieth day of June to die I was condemned.
And now I'm at the scaffold to bid you all adieu,
The hangman now is waiting, it's a quarter after two;
The black cap is on my face, no longer can I see,
But when I'm dead and buried, dear Lord, remember me.

Image of presidential assassin Charles Guiteau, on the cover of Puck *magazine.* Library of Congress Prints and Photographs Division

Portrait of Pres. Chester A. Arthur. During his short administration, Arthur won the respect of political skeptics, but not the renomination bid of his party in 1884. National Archives/ Getty Images

Arthur's accession to the presidency caused widespread concern. He had held no elective office before becoming vice president, and he had been closely associated with the Stalwart wing of the party. It was assumed that, like others in that group, he would be hostile to civil service reform, and his nomination for the vice presidency had been generally regarded as a deliberate rebuke to President Hayes. The members of Garfield's cabinet immediately tendered their resignations, but Arthur asked them to continue in office for a time. By mid-April 1882, however, all but one of the cabinet officers had been replaced.

Arthur soon surprised his critics and the country by demonstrating an unexpected independence of his former political friends. In his first annual message to Congress, in December 1881, he announced his qualified approval of legislation that would remove appointments to the federal civil service from partisan control. In January 1883 Congress passed and Arthur signed the Pendleton Civil Service Act, which established the Civil Service Commission and provided that appointments to certain categories of offices should be made on the basis of examinations and the appointees given an indefinite tenure in their positions.

By 1884, when the next presidential election was held, Arthur's administration had won the respect of many who had viewed his accession to office with misgivings. It had not, however, gained him any strong following among the leaders of his party. The foremost candidate for the Republican nomination was the perennially powerful Blaine, who, despite opposition from those who believed he was too partisan in spirit or that he was vulnerable to charges of corrupt actions while speaker of the house many years before, was nominated on the fourth ballot.

The Democratic candidate, Gov. Grover Cleveland of New York, was in many respects the antithesis of Blaine. He was a relative newcomer to politics. He had been elected mayor of Buffalo in 1881 and governor of New York in 1882.

In both positions he had earned a reputation for political independence, inflexible honesty, and an industrious and conservative administration. His record made him an attractive candidate for those who accepted the dictum that "a public office is a public trust." This was, in 1884, a valuable asset; it won for Cleveland the support of a few outstanding Republicans and some journals of national circulation that usually favoured Republican nominees for office.

As in 1880, the campaign was almost devoid of issues of public policy. Only the perennial question of the tariff appeared to separate the two parties. Cleveland had not served in the army during the Civil War, and Republicans made an effort to use this fact, together with the power of the South in the Democratic Party, to arouse sectional prejudices against Cleveland. During the campaign it was revealed that Cleveland, a bachelor, was the father of an illegitimate son, an indiscretion that gave the Republicans a moral issue with which to counteract charges of corruption against their own candidate.

The election was very close. On the evening of the voting it was apparent that the result depended upon the vote in New York state, but not until the end of the week was it certain that Cleveland had carried New York by the narrow margin of some 1,100 votes (out of more than 1 million) and been elected president.

CHAPTER 8

GROVER CLEVELAND'S FIRST TERM

Grover Cleveland was the first Democratic president since James Buchanan a quarter of a century earlier. More than two-thirds of the electoral votes he received came from Southern or border states, so that it appeared that his election marked the close of one epoch and the beginning of a new political era in which the South could again hope to have a major voice in the conduct of national affairs. Because of his brief career in politics, Cleveland had only a limited acquaintance with leaders of his own party. He accepted literally the constitutional principle of the separation of powers, and he opened his first annual message to Congress, in December 1885, with an affirmation of his devotion to "the partitions of power between our respective departments." This appeared to be a disavowal of presidential leadership, but it quickly became apparent that Cleveland intended to defend vigorously the prerogatives that he believed belonged to the executive.

During his first term (1885–89) Cleveland was confronted with a divided Congress—a Republican Senate and a Democratic House. This added to the complexities of administration, especially in the matter of appointments. Cleveland was a firm believer in a civil service based on merit rather than on partisan considerations, but, as the first Democratic president in a quarter of a century, he was under great pressure to replace Republicans in appointive offices with Democrats. He followed a line of compromise. In his first two years he removed the incumbents from about two-thirds of the offices subject to his control, but he scrutinized the qualifications of Democrats recommended for appointment and in a number of instances refused to abide by the recommendations of his party leaders. He thus offended both the reformers, who wished no partisan removals, and his fellow Democrats, whose nominees he rejected. Although his handling of the patronage alienated some powerful Democrats, he scored a personal triumph when he persuaded Congress to repeal the obsolete Tenure of Office Act of 1867, which Republican senators had threatened to revive in order to embarrass him.

Cleveland was a conservative on all matters relating to money, and he was inflexibly opposed to wasteful expenditure of public funds. This caused him to investigate as many as possible of the hundreds of private bills passed by Congress to compensate private individuals, usually Federal veterans, for claims against the federal government. When, as was frequently the case, he judged these claims to be ill-founded, he vetoed the bill. He was the first president to use the veto

Pres. Grover Cleveland. A divided Congress and alienation due to his handling of partisan appointments were but two of the hurdles facing Cleveland during his administration. Library of Congress Prints and Photographs Division

power extensively to block the enactment of this type of private legislation.

THE SURPLUS AND THE TARIFF

The flurry of private pension bills had been stimulated, in part, by a growing surplus in the Treasury. In every year since the Civil War, there had been an excess of revenue over expenditures, a circumstance that encouraged suggestions for appropriations of public funds for a variety of purposes. The surplus also focused attention upon the tariff, the principal source of this excess revenue. In 1883 Congress had reviewed the tariff and made numerous changes in the rates, increasing the tariff on some items and reducing it on others, without materially decreasing the revenue received. Cleveland believed that the surplus presented a very real problem. It hoarded in the Treasury money that could have been in circulation, and it encouraged reckless spending by the government. Like many other Democrats, he disliked the high protective tariff. After waiting in vain for two years for Congress to meet this issue boldly, Cleveland adopted the extraordinary tactic of devoting his entire annual message in 1887 to a discussion of this question and to an appeal for a lowering of the tariff. The House then passed a bill generally conforming to Cleveland's views on the tariff but the Senate rejected it, and the tariff became a leading issue in the presidential campaign of 1888.

THE PUBLIC DOMAIN

After 1877 hundreds of thousands of agricultural settlers went westward to the Plains, where they came into competition for control of the land with the cattlemen, who hitherto had dominated the open range. The pressure of population as it moved into the Plains called attention to the diminishing supply of good, arable land still open to settlement, thus

presaging the day when there would no longer be a vast reservoir of land in the West awaiting the farmer. It also drew attention to the fact that millions of acres of Western land were being held for speculative purposes, and that other millions of acres had been acquired by questionable means or were still in the possession of railroads that had failed to fulfill the obligations they had assumed when the land had been granted to them. Upon assuming office, Cleveland was confronted with evidence that some of these claims had been fraudulently obtained by railroads, speculators, cattlemen, or lumbering interests. He ordered an investigation, and for more than a year agents of the Land Office roamed over the West uncovering evidence of irregularities and neglected obligations. Cleveland acted firmly. By executive orders and court action he succeeded in restoring more than 81 million acres (33 million hectares) to the public domain.

THE INTERSTATE COMMERCE ACT

The railroads were vital to the country's economy, but because a single company enjoyed a monopoly of rail transportation in so many regions, many of the railroads adopted policies that large numbers of their customers felt to be unfair and discriminatory. Before 1884 it was clear that the Granger laws of the preceding decade (state laws prohibiting various

A cartoon showing railroad tycoons divvying up the United States into regional monopolies.
Stock Montage/Archive Photos/Getty Images

abuses by the railroads) were ineffective, and pressure groups turned to the federal government for relief. In this, Western farm organizations were joined by influential Eastern businessmen who believed that they, too, were the victims of discrimination by the railroads. This powerful political alliance persuaded both parties to include regulation of the railroads in their national platforms in 1884 and induced Congress to enact the Interstate Commerce Act in 1887.

This law, designed to prevent unjust discrimination by the railroads, prohibited the pooling of traffic and profits, made it illegal for a railroad to charge more for a short haul than for a longer one, required that the roads publicize their rates, and established the Interstate Commerce Commission to supervise the enforcement of the law. The rulings of the commission were subject to review by the federal courts, the decisions of which tended to narrow the scope of the act. The commission was less effective than the sponsors of the act had hoped, but the act in itself was an indication of the growing realization that only the federal government could cope with the new economic problems of the day.

THE ELECTION OF 1888

Cleveland's plea for a reduction of the tariff in his annual message of 1887 made it certain that the tariff would be the central issue in the presidential campaign of 1888. The Democrats renominated Cleveland, although it was thought that he had endangered his chances of reelection by his outspoken advocacy of tariff reduction. The Republicans had their usual difficulty in selecting a candidate. Blaine refused to enter the race, and no other person in the party commanded substantial support. From among the

Document: Grover Cleveland: Surplus Revenues and the Tariff (1887)

Pres. Grover Cleveland's third annual message to Congress, on Dec. 6, 1887, called for tariff reductions. Since the federal surplus was annually over $100 million, and prices on commodities were kept artificially high by import taxes, the president believed the time was right for Congress to reduce the tariff on many items. A portion of his message appears below.

You are confronted at the threshold of your legislative duties with a condition of the national finances which imperatively demands immediate and careful consideration.

The amount of money annually exacted, through the operation of present laws, from the industries and necessities of the people largely exceeds the sum necessary to meet the expenses of the government. When we consider that the theory of our institutions guarantees to every citizen the full enjoyment of all the fruits of his industry and enterprise, with only such deduction as may be his share toward the careful and economical maintenance of the government which protects him, it is plain that the exaction of more than this is indefensible extortion and a culpable betrayal of American fairness and justice. This wrong inflicted upon those who bear the burden of national taxation, like other wrongs, multiplies a brood of evil consequences.

The public Treasury, which should only exist as a conduit conveying the people's tribute to its legitimate objects of expenditure, becomes a hoarding place for money needlessly withdrawn from trade and the people's use, thus crippling our national energies, suspending our country's development, preventing investment in productive enterprise, threatening financial disturbance; and inviting schemes of public plunder. This condition of our Treasury is not altogether new, and it has more than once of late been submitted to the people's representatives in the Congress, who alone can apply a remedy. And yet the situation still continues; with aggravated incidents, more than ever presaging financial convulsion and widespread disaster.

It will not do to neglect this situation because its dangers are not now palpably imminent and apparent. They exist nonetheless certainly, and await the unforeseen and unexpected occasion when suddenly they will be precipitated upon us....

An 1888 presidential election poster for Grover Cleveland and Allen G. Thurman highlighting the Democratic ticket's emphasis on tariff reduction. Cleveland lost to Benjamin Harrison by a slim margin. Buyenlarge/Archive Photos/Getty Images

many who were willing to accept the nomination, the Republicans selected Benjamin Harrison of Indiana, a Union general in the Civil War and the grandson of Pres. William Henry Harrison.

Cleveland had won respect as a man of integrity and courage, but neither he nor Harrison aroused any great enthusiasm among the voters. One feature of the campaign noted by observers was the extensive use of money to influence the outcome. This was not a new phenomenon, but the spending of money to carry doubtful states and the apparent alliance between business and political bosses had never before been so open.

The results were again close. Cleveland had a plurality of about 100,000 popular votes, but the Republicans carried two states, New York and Indiana, which they had lost in 1884. In the electoral college, Harrison won by a margin of 233 to 168.

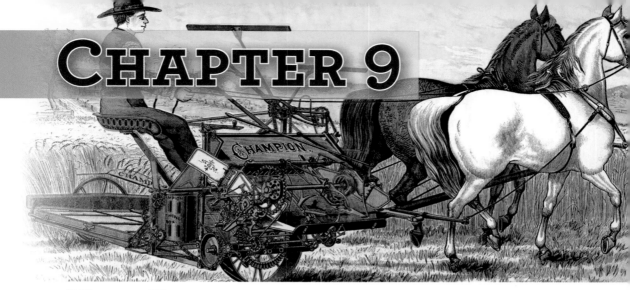

CHAPTER 9

THE BENJAMIN HARRISON ADMINISTRATION

The Republicans also gained control of both houses of the 51st Congress. Their margin in the House of Representatives, however, was so small that it seemed uncertain whether they could carry controversial legislation through it. This obstacle was overcome by the speaker of the House, Thomas B. Reed of Maine. Reed refused to recognize dilatory motions and, contrary to precedent, he counted as present all members who were in the chamber. Using that tactic, he ruled, on occasion, that a quorum was present even though fewer than a majority had actually answered a roll call. His iron rule of the House earned him the sobriquet Czar Reed, but only through his firm control of the House could the Republicans pass three controversial bills in the summer and early autumn of 1890. One dealt with monopolies, another with silver, and the third with the tariff.

THE SHERMAN ANTI-TRUST ACT

The first of these major measures declared illegal all combinations that restrained trade between states or with foreign countries. This law, known as the Sherman Anti-Trust Act, was passed by Congress early in July. It was the congressional response to evidence of growing public dissatisfaction with the development of industrial monopolies, which had been so notable a feature of the preceding decade.

More than 10 years passed before the Sherman Act was used to break up any industrial monopoly. It was invoked by the federal government in 1894 to obtain an injunction against a striking railroad union accused of restraint of interstate commerce, and the use of the injunction was upheld by the Supreme Court in 1895. Indeed, it is unlikely that the Senate would have passed the bill in 1890 had not the chairman of the Senate Judiciary Committee, George F. Edmunds of Vermont, felt certain that unions were combinations in restraint of trade within the meaning of the law.

To those who hoped that the Sherman Act would inhibit the growth of monopoly, the results were disappointing. The passage of the act only three years after the Interstate Commerce Act was, however, another sign that the public was turning from state capitals to Washington for effective regulation of industrial giants.

THE SILVER ISSUE

Less than two weeks after Congress passed the antitrust law, it enacted the

Soldiers stand watch over trains in Chicago during the 1894 Pullman railroad strike. The Sherman Anti-Trust Act, passed a decade earlier, was used to break the strike. Kean Collection/Archive Photos/Getty Images

Document: The Sherman Anti-Trust Act (1890)

The enormous success of the Standard Oil Trust stimulated similar agreements in other American industries in the 1870s and 1880s. After state attempts to control the growth of monopolies had proved ineffective, some federal restraint was provided by passage of the Sherman Antitrust Act of 1890. The act was inadequate in that it did not define "trusts," provide for practical means of "restraint," or indicate whether labor combinations, as well as industrial, were to be subject to its provisions. The vagueness of the act itself, plus subsequent Supreme Court rulings, deprived it of any real effectiveness against the trusts, although it was used effectively against labour organizations on several occasions.

Section 1. Every contract, combination in the form of trust or otherwise, or conspiracy in restraint of trade or commerce among the several states or with foreign nations is hereby declared to be illegal. Every person who shall make any such contract or engage in any such combination or conspiracy shall be deemed guilty of a misdemeanor, and on conviction thereof shall be punished by fine not exceeding $5,000 or by imprisonment not exceeding one year, or by both said punishments, in the discretion of the court.

Section 2. Every person who shall monopolize, or attempt to monopolize, or combine or conspire with any other person or persons to monopolize any part of the trade or commerce among the several states or with foreign nations shall be deemed guilty of a misdemeanor, and on conviction thereof shall be punished by fine not exceeding $5,000 or by imprisonment not exceeding one year, or by both said punishments, in the discretion of the court....

Sherman Silver Purchase Act, which required the secretary of the treasury to purchase each month 4.5 million ounces (130,000 kilograms) of silver at the market price. This act superseded the Bland–Allison Act of 1878, effectively increasing the government's monthly purchase of silver by more than 50 percent. It was adopted in response to pressure from mineowners, who were alarmed by the falling price of silver, and Western farmers, who were always favourable to inflationary measures and who, in 1890, were also suffering from the depressed prices of their products.

THE MCKINLEY TARIFF

Most Republican leaders had been lukewarm concerning the proposal to increase the purchase of silver and had accepted it only to assure Western votes for the measure in which they were most interested—upward revision of the protective tariff. This was accomplished in the McKinley Tariff Act of October 1890, passed by Congress one month before the midterm elections of that year. The tariff was designed to appeal to the farmers because some agricultural products were added to the protected list. A few items, notably sugar, were placed on the free list, and domestic sugar planters were to be compensated by a subsidy of 2 cents a pound. The central feature of the act, however, was a general increase in tariff schedules, with many of these increases applying to items of general consumption.

The new tariff immediately became an issue in the congressional elections. It failed to halt the downward spiral of farm prices, but there was an almost immediate increase in the cost of many items purchased by the farmers. With discontent already rife in the agricultural regions of the West and South, the McKinley tariff added to agrarian resentment. The outcome of the elections was a major defeat for the Republicans, whose strength in the House of Representatives was reduced by almost half.

THE AGRARIAN REVOLT

Political disaster befell the Republicans in the trans-Mississippi West, resulting from an economic and psychological depression that enveloped the region after widespread crop failures and the collapse of inflated land prices in the summer of 1887. The Western boom had begun in the late 1870s, when the tide of migration into the unoccupied farmlands beyond the Mississippi quickly led to the settlement of hitherto unoccupied parts of Iowa and Minnesota and to the pushing of the frontier westward across the Plains almost literally to the shadows of the Rocky Mountains.

Westward expansion was encouraged by the railroads that served the region. It was supported by the satisfactory price and encouraging foreign market for wheat, the money crop of the Plains. For 10 years, from 1877 through 1886, the farmers on the Plains had the benefit of an abnormally generous rainfall, leading many to assume that climatic conditions had changed and that the rain belt had moved westward to provide adequate rainfall for the Plains. Confidence was followed by unrestrained optimism that engendered wild speculation and a rise in land prices. Lured on by these illusions, the settlers went into debt to make improvements on their farms while small-town leaders dreamed of prodigious growth and authorized bond issues to construct the public improvements they felt certain would soon be needed.

The collapse of these dreams came in 1887. The year opened ominously when the Plains were swept by a catastrophic blizzard in January that killed thousands of head of cattle and virtually destroyed the cattle industry of the open range. The following summer was dry and hot; crops were poor; and, to compound the woes of the farmers, the price of wheat began to slide downward. The dry summer of 1887 was the beginning of a 10-year cycle of little rainfall and searingly hot summers. By the autumn of 1887 the exodus from the Plains had begun; five years later, areas of western Kansas and Nebraska that had once been thriving agricultural centres were almost depopulated. The agricultural regions east of the Plains were less

Homesteaders stand outside their cabin in 1889 Oklahoma. Some 100,000 Americans laid claim to land in the rush to settle the Oklahoma Territory. Hulton Archive/Getty Images

directly affected, though there the farmers suffered from the general decline in farm prices.

Although the disaster on the Plains bred a sense of distress and frustration, the lure of good land was still strong. When the central portion of the present state of Oklahoma was opened to settlement in April 1889, an army of eager settlers, estimated to have numbered 100,000, rushed into the district to claim homesteads and build homes.

THE POPULISTS

The collapse of the boom and the falling prices of agricultural products forced many farmers to seek relief through political action. In 1888, and again in 1890, this discontent was expressed through local political groups, commonly known as Farmers' Alliances, which quickly spread through parts of the West and in the South, where economic problems had been aggravated by the shift following the Civil War from a plantation system to sharecrop and crop-lien systems. The alliances won some local victories and contributed to the discomfiture of the Republicans in 1890. They were not, however, an effective vehicle for concerted political action; in 1891 the leaders of the alliances formed the People's (Populist) Party.

Document: Hamilton Wicks: The Oklahoma Land Rush (1889)

The "unassigned lands" of the Oklahoma Territory encompassed approximately 2 million acres near the centre of the state not occupied by the Cherokee, Chickasaw, Choctaw, Creek, and Seminole nations. When these lands were opened to settlement under the terms of the Homestead Act, an estimated 100,000 people started out at noon on April 22, 1889, to vie for the tracts (160 acres to a person) of free land. Hamilton Wicks participated in the famous "land rush" and recorded the following account of that chaotic scene.

A city established and populated in half a day, in a remote region of country and many miles distant from the nearest civilized community, is a marvel that could have been possible in no age but our own, and in no land except the United States.

The opening of Oklahoma was indeed one of the most important events that has occurred in the development of the West. It marks an epoch in the settlement of the unoccupied lands owned by the government of the United States. Never before has there been such a general uprising of the common people seeking homesteads upon the few remaining acres possessed by Uncle Sam. The conditions and circumstances of the settlement of Oklahoma were widely different from those of the settlement of any other section of the United States. This new territory is surrounded by thoroughly settled and well-organized commonwealths. It is a region containing an area of 69,000 square miles, having an average width of 470 miles, and an average length of 210 miles, being much larger than Ohio, or Indiana, or Kentucky, or Illinois, or "the Virginias," or even the whole of New England.

No method can so clearly bring before the public the actual facts of this wonderful opening as the narration, by one who participated in it, of his experience....

The Populists aspired to become a national party and hoped to attract support from labour, and from reform groups generally. In practice, however, they continued through their brief career to be almost wholly a party of Western farmers. (Southern farmers, afraid of splitting the white vote and thereby allowing blacks into power, largely remained loyal to the Democratic Party.) The Populists demanded an increase in the circulating currency, to be achieved by the unlimited coinage of silver, a graduated income tax, government ownership of the railroads, a tariff for revenue only, the direct election of U.S. senators, and other measures designed to strengthen political democracy and give the farmers economic parity with business and industry. In 1892 the Populists nominated Gen. James B. Weaver of Iowa for president.

THE ELECTION OF 1892

The nominees of the two major parties for president in 1892 were the same as in the election of 1888, Harrison and Cleveland. The unpopularity of the McKinley tariff gave Cleveland an advantage, as did the discontent in the West, which was directed

A Populist movement rally being held in Kansas. The movement, composed of members from several farmers' organizations, sought economic and tariff reform. Fotosearch/Archive Photos/ Getty Images

largely against the Republican Party. From the beginning of the campaign it appeared probable that the Democrats would be successful. Cleveland carried not only the Southern states but also such key Northern states as New York and Illinois. His electoral vote was 277 to 145 for Harrison. Weaver carried only four Western states, three of them states with important silver mines, and received 22 electoral votes.

Document: William A. Peffer: The Rise of Farmer Organizations (1891)

Organized efforts to improve the lot of farmers flourished in the Mississippi Valley during the 1860s and 1870s. But groups such as the Grange and Farmers' Alliances fell victim to their own accomplishments and declined as conditions improved. The settlement of the Great Plains, however, brought new problems with taxes, land prices, and exorbitant fees charged by middlemen for procuring loans and selling crops; in Kansas alone, 11,000 mortgages were foreclosed between 1889 and 1893. These frustrations soon gave rise to new calls to organize for mutual assistance. The following account by Sen. William A. Peffer of Kansas appeared in 1891.

The Grange

The Patrons of Husbandry, commonly known as the Grange, began their organization about twenty-four years ago in the city of Washington. The Grange grew rapidly about nine years, then quite as rapidly for a time receded from view; but in the meantime it had accomplished a noble work, much wider in its scope and grander in its proportions than people generally have ever been willing to admit. From the Grange came what is known as the "Granger" railroad legislation, the establishment in our laws of the principle that transportation belongs to the people, that it is a matter for the people themselves to manage in their own way, and that the Congress of the United States, under authority vested in that body by the Constitution, is authorized and empowered to regulate commerce among the several states as well as with foreign nations. That principle, once advocated and urged by the Grange, finally became permanently ingrafted in our laws.

Then came the Interstate Commerce Commission; that was another outcome of the Grange movement. Opposition to conspiracies of wealth against the rights of farmers—of labor in general, but of farmers in particular—was among the first and best works of the Grange. The footprints of that first and best organization of farmers ever effected up to that time—are seen plainly in much of the legislation of this country during the last twenty years. Grange influence revived in recent years, and is again growing. It is now one of the most earnest, active, and efficient agencies in the agitation of measures in the interest of agriculture. It lacks but one element of strength, and that will come in due time—namely, the uniting with other bodies of organized farmers in one great political movement to enforce themselves what they have long been trying ineffectually to enforce through their separate party organizations—the dethronement of the money power....

World's Columbian Exposition

As the 400th anniversary of Christopher Columbus's voyage to America approached, there was a spirited competition among the country's leading cities to host a fair to commemorate the historic event in 1893. Chicago was chosen in part because it was a railroad centre and in part because it offered a guarantee of $10 million.

Continuing the precedent set at the Philadelphia Centennial Exposition (1876) of creating a vast gardened layout containing numerous separate buildings rather than a single great hall, the World's Columbian Exposition was planned to spread over 686 acres (278 hectares) along the city's south lakefront area; part of this location is now Jackson Park in Chicago. The chief planner was the Chicago architect Daniel H. Burnham, Charles B. Atwood was designer in chief, and Frederick Law Olmsted was entrusted with landscaping. The fair's new buildings had impressive Classical facades with a uniform cornice height of 60 feet (18.25 metres). The plaster palace fronts bore little functional relationship to exhibition halls inside, but the grandeur of the "White City," electrically lighted at night, temporarily led to a resurgent interest in Classical architecture.

Bird's-eye view of the 1893 World's Columbian Exposition, Chicago; lithograph by Currier and Ives. Library of Congress, Washington, D.C. (neg. no. LC-USZC2-3394)

Behind the calm pillared facades and Classical porticoes of the great "White City" the visitor found unexpected excitement and novelty. The Ferris wheel (invented by G.W.G. Ferris, a Pittsburgh engineer) and a dazzling new wonder—electricity—were presented for the first time in America. Electricity had been introduced and exploited at the Paris Exposition of 1889, but in 1893 it was still unfamiliar to most Americans. The exposition was opened by a dramatic act when Pres. Grover Cleveland pushed a button in the White House and set the great Allis engine in motion in Chicago, turning on the electric power for the exposition. The engine, the dynamo, and

The original Ferris wheel, designed by George Washington Gale Ferris, built for the World's Columbian Exposition, Chicago, 1893. Library of Congress, Washington, D.C. (digital id: cph 3a50979u)

the alternating-current generator displayed for the first time by George Westinghouse later became the basic tools of the electric power industry.

The Columbian Exposition's gross outlays amounted to $28,340,700, of which $18,678,000 was spent on grounds and buildings. There were some 21.5 million paid admissions to the exposition, and actual total attendance (including free admissions) was more than 25.8 million. However, because some visitors were counted twice, the total figure is sometimes reported as having been between 27 million and 28 million. The cash balance remaining at closing was $446,832 making it the first American international exposition to close with a profit. The Palace of Fine Arts, a 600,000-square-foot building, was rebuilt in permanent limestone in 1928–32 to house the public exhibitions of the Museum of Science and Industry.

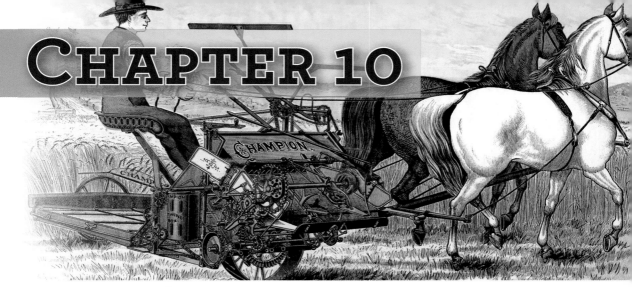

CHAPTER 10

FROM CLEVELAND TO ECONOMIC RECOVERY

The 22nd president of the United States had become the 24th president of the United States, marking the first time a president had ever served discontinuous terms. The challenges facing Pres. Grover Cleveland in his second term were considerable. Yet Cleveland continued to distinguish himself as one of the few truly honest and principled politicians of the Gilded Age.

CLEVELAND'S SECOND TERM

When he was inaugurated for his second term in March 1893, the country hovered on the brink of financial panic. Six years of depression in the trans-Mississippi West, the decline of foreign trade after the enactment of the McKinley tariff, and an abnormally high burden of private debt were disquieting features of the situation. Most attention was centred, however, on the gold reserve in the federal Treasury. It was assumed that a minimum reserve of $100,000,000 was necessary to assure redemption of government obligations in gold. When on April 21, 1893, the reserve fell below that amount, the psychological impact was far-reaching. Investors hastened to convert their holdings into gold; banks and brokerage houses were hard-pressed; and many business houses and financial institutions failed. Prices dropped, employment was curtailed, and the nation entered a period of severe economic depression that continued for more than three years.

The causes of this disaster were numerous and complex, but the attention that focused on the gold reserve tended to concentrate concern upon a single factor—the restoration of the Treasury's supply of gold. It was widely believed that the principal cause of the drain on the Treasury was the obligation to purchase large amounts of silver. To those who held this view, the obvious remedy was the repeal of the Sherman Silver Purchase Act.

The issue was political as well as economic. It divided both major parties, but most of the leading advocates of existing silver policies were Democrats. Cleveland, however, had long been opposed to the silver-purchase policy, and in the crisis he resolved upon repeal as an essential step in protecting the Treasury. He therefore called Congress to meet in special session on Aug. 7, 1893.

The new Congress had Democratic majorities in both houses, and, if it had any mandate, it was to repeal the McKinley tariff. It had no mandate on the silver issue, and more than half of its Democratic members came from constituencies that favoured an increase in the coinage of silver. Cleveland faced a herculean task in forcing repeal through Congress, but, by the use of every power at his command, he gained his objective. The Sherman Silver Purchase Act was repealed at the end of

Document: James Laurence Laughlin: Against Free Coinage of Silver (1895)

The Populist Party, outraged by President Cleveland's repeal of the Sherman Silver Purchase Act in 1893, propagandized continuously on the virtues of free silver. The party accepted the formula proposed by one of its most effective spokesmen, W. H. "Coin" Harvey, and proclaimed that farmers and workers would benefit greatly by adopting the coinage of silver at a ratio of 16 to 1 (of gold). "The bimetallic standard," Harvey declared, "will make the United States the most prosperous nation on the globe." James Laughlin, a professor of political economy at the University of Chicago and one of the staunchest critics of free silver, debated the issue with Harvey in 1895. Laughlin's views are reprinted here.

Money is used as a common denominator to which other things are referred for comparison. In order to compare goods with money, there is no more need of as many pieces of money as there are articles to be compared than there is of having a quart cup for every quart of milk in existence, or of having a yardstick in a dry goods store for every yard of cloth on the shelf. The idea that it is necessary to multiply the measurements of value is absurd; but it is of the foremost importance that the measure of values should not be tampered with and should not be changed by legislation to the damage of all transactions based upon it. Right here is the whole secret of the opposition to silver as money. Silver has lost its stability of value. It is no better than any ordinary metal for stability. The action of India in June 1893 sends it down 20 percent. The mere rumor of the Chinese indemnity sends it up 10 percent.

The greater or less quantity of money there is roaming about in circulation is no reason why anyone gets more of it. Money, like property, is parted with for a consideration. No matter how many more coins there are coming from the mint under free coinage and going into the vaults of the banks to the credit of the mine owners who own the bullion, there are no more coins in the pockets of Weary Waggles, who is cooling his heels on the sidewalk outside the bank....

Document: Jacob S. Coxey: Business Depression and Public Works (1894)

Jacob Coxey was one of the more colourful figures of the Populist movement of the 1890s. "Coxey's Army," 100 strong and accompanied by half that many newspapermen, set off from Massillon, Ohio, on Easter Sunday 1894. The group of unemployed numbered 500, rather than the hoped for 100,000, when they reached Washington, D.C., for a May Day demonstration. The march disintegrated when Coxey was arrested for trying to speak from the Capitol steps and jailed for trespassing on the Capitol lawn, but the effort inspired other marches and was symptomatic of the unrest among workers.

Coxey wanted to dramatize a proposal (written in the form of a congressional bill) that the federal government ease the depression that followed the Panic of 1893 by issuing legal tender currency to pay for the building of roads, thereby providing work for the unemployed. Coxey's "bills" are reprinted below.

THE BILL...TO BUILD GOOD ROADS...

Section 1. Be it enacted by the Senate and House of Representatives in Congress assembled, that the secretary of the Treasury of the United States is hereby authorized and instructed to have engraved and printed, immediately after the passage of this bill, $500 million of Treasury notes, a legal tender for all debts, public and private, said notes to be in denominations of $1, $2, $5, and $10; and to be placed in a fund to be known as the General County Road Fund System of the United States, and to be expended solely for said purpose.

Section 2. And be it further enacted, that it shall be the duty of the secretary of war to take charge of the construction of the said General County Road System in the United States, and said construction to commence as soon as the secretary of the Treasury shall inform the secretary of war that the said fund is available, which shall not be later than ———; when it shall be the duty of the secretary of war to inaugurate the work and expend the sum of $20 million per month, pro rata, with the number of miles of roads in each state and territory in the United States.

Section 3. Be it further enacted, that all labor other than that of the secretary of war, "whose compensations are already fixed by law," shall be paid by the day, and that the rate be not less than $1.50 per day for common labor and $3.50 per day for team and labor; and that eight hours per day shall constitute a day's labor under the provisions of this bill....

Jacob Coxey's "Army" of unemployed marching to Washington, D.C., from Massillon, Ohio, to petition the government to pass legislation for relief of the depression that followed the Panic of 1893. Library of Congress, Washington, D.C.

October by a bill that made no compensating provision for the coinage of silver. Cleveland had won a personal triumph, but he had irrevocably divided his party; and in some sections of the nation he had become the most unpopular president of his generation.

The extent to which Cleveland had lost control of his party became apparent when Congress turned from silver to the tariff. The House passed a bill that would have revised tariff rates downward in accordance with the president's views. In the Senate, however, the bill was so altered that it bore little resemblance to the original measure, and on some items it imposed higher duties than had the McKinley Tariff Act. It was finally passed in August 1894, but Cleveland was so dissatisfied that he refused to sign it; the bill became law without his signature. The act contained a provision for an income tax, but this feature was declared unconstitutional by the Supreme Court in 1895.

In the midterm elections of 1894 the Republicans recaptured control of both houses of Congress. This indicated the discontent produced by the continuing depression. It also guaranteed that, with a Democratic president and Republican Congress, there would be inaction in domestic legislation while both parties looked forward to the election of 1896.

THE ELECTION OF 1896

At their convention in St. Louis the Republicans selected Gov. William McKinley of Ohio as their presidential nominee. He had served in the Union army during the Civil War, and his record as governor of Ohio tended to offset his association with the unpopular tariff of 1890. His most effective support in winning the nomination, however, was provided by Mark Hanna, a wealthy Cleveland businessman who was McKinley's closest friend.

Mark Hanna

The prosperous owner of a Cleveland coal and iron enterprise, Mark Hanna (born Marcus Alonzo Hanna on Sept. 24, 1837) soon expanded his interests to include banking, transportation, and publishing. Convinced that the welfare of business (and consequently the prosperity of the country) was dependent upon the success of the Republican Party, he began as early as 1880 to work among industrialists to ensure the financial support of likely candidates for office. He was especially impressed by Ohio congressman William McKinley's successful sponsorship in 1890 of a high protective tariff, and thenceforth he devoted all his energies to McKinley's political advancement, first as governor (1892–96) and then as president (1897–1901).

In preparation for the 1896 contest with the Democrat-Populist candidate, William Jennings Bryan, Hanna was reputed to have poured more than $100,000 of his own money into preconvention expenses alone. Raising an unprecedented fund from wealthy individuals and corporations, the dynamic Hanna skillfully directed the $3.5 million campaign—the costliest and best organized the nation had ever witnessed. At a rate of spending exceeding his opponents by 20 to 1, his 1,400 paid workers inundated the country with millions of pamphlets promising continuing prosperity with McKinley. Hanna succeeded in stunting Bryan's grassroots appeal with a continual barrage of posters and propaganda that preceded and followed Bryan at every whistle-stop of his campaign train.

Once in office, McKinley helped to fulfill Hanna's lifelong ambition by appointing Sen. John Sherman secretary of state, thus creating a vacancy in the U.S. Senate. Hanna was elected to fill the vacancy (March 1897) and remained in the Senate until his death.

Industrialist and political kingmaker Mark Hanna. Library of Congress Prints and Photographs Division

The youngest man ever to receive a major party's presidential nomination, William Jennings Bryan largely supported agrarian interests. MPI/Archive Photos/Getty Images

The Democratic convention in Chicago was unusually exciting. It was controlled by groups hostile to Cleveland's financial policies, and it took the unprecedented step of rejecting a resolution commending the administration of a president of its own party. The debate on the party platform featured an eloquent defense of silver and agrarian interests by William Jennings Bryan, which won him not only a prolonged ovation but also his party's presidential nomination. Bryan was a former congressman from Nebraska, and, at 36, he was the youngest man ever to become the nominee for president of a major party. By experience and conviction he shared the outlook of the agrarian elements that dominated the convention and whose principal spokesman he became.

Bryan conducted a vigorous campaign. For the first time a presidential candidate carried his case to the people in all parts of the country, and for a time it appeared that he might win. The worried conservatives charged that Bryan was a dangerous demagogue, and they interpreted the campaign as a conflict between defenders of a sound economic system that would produce prosperity and dishonest radicals who championed reckless innovations that would undermine the financial security of the nation. On this interpretation they succeeded in raising large campaign funds from industrialists who feared their interests were threatened. With this money, the Republicans were able to turn the tide and win a decisive victory. Outside the South, Bryan carried only the Western silver states, as well as Kansas and Nebraska.

ECONOMIC RECOVERY

Soon after taking office on March 4, 1897, McKinley called Congress into special session to revise the tariff once again. Congress responded by passing the Dingley Tariff Act, which eliminated many items from the free list and generally raised duties on imports to the highest level they had yet reached.

Although the preservation of the gold standard had been the chief appeal of the Republicans in 1896, it was not until March 1900 that Congress enacted the Gold Standard Act, which required the Treasury to maintain a minimum gold reserve of $150 million, and authorized the issuance of bonds, if necessary, to protect that minimum. In 1900 such a measure was almost anticlimactic, for an adequate gold supply had ceased to be a

Document: William Jennings Bryan: The Cross of Gold (1896)

"We are unalterably opposed," declared the Republican Party platform in 1896, "to every measure calculated to debase our currency." A few weeks later the Democratic Party platform demanded "the free and unlimited coinage of both silver and gold." Thus a major debate on the currency issue seemed likely when, as the final speaker in defense of the Democratic platform, young William Jennings Bryan not only made it inevitable but also electrified the convention with his eloquent plea for the coinage of silver. His concluding sentence, "You shall not crucify mankind upon a cross of gold," became the battle cry of the silver Democrats and is one of the most famous American political statements. Bryan's speech, delivered on July 8, 1896, catapulted him into a position of leadership in his party and won him its presidential nomination.

I would be presumptuous, indeed, to present myself against the distinguished gentlemen to whom you have listened if this were but a measuring of ability; but this is not a contest among persons. The humblest citizen in all the land when clad in armor of a righteous cause is stronger than all the whole hosts of error that they can bring. I come to speak to you in defense of a cause as holy as the cause of liberty—the cause of humanity. When this debate is concluded, a motion will be made to lay upon the table the resolution offered in commendation of the administration and also the resolution in condemnation of the administration. I shall object to bringing this question down to a level of persons. The individual is but an atom; he is born, he acts, he dies; but principles are eternal; and this has been a contest of principle.

Never before in the history of this country has there been witnessed such a contest as that through which we have passed. Never before in the history of American politics has a great issue been fought out as this issue has been by the voters themselves....

practical problem. Beginning in 1893, the production of gold in the United States had increased steadily; by 1899 the annual value of gold added to the American supply was double that of any year between 1881 and 1892. The chief source of the new supply of gold was the Klondike, where important deposits of gold had been discovered during the summer of 1896.

By 1898 the depression had run its course. Farm prices and the volume of farm exports were again rising steadily, and Western farmers appeared to forget their recent troubles and regain confidence in their economic prospects. In industry, the return of prosperity was marked by a resumption of the move toward more industrial combinations, despite the antitrust law. Great banking houses, such as J.P. Morgan and Company of New York, played a key role in many of the most important of these combinations by providing the necessary capital and receiving, in return, an influential voice in the management of the companies created by this capital.

The era between the Civil War and the turn of the 20th century in the United States was marked by the emergence of both big business and big labour, the struggle between big ideas, and the dominance of big personalities, though few of the last occupied the White House. Huge fortunes were made and lavishly spent, while at the same time workers fought for a fair wage and an eight-hour day. Strikes were, for a time, ubiquitous; clashes were inevitable. "Captains of industry" faced off with Knights of Labor. Through trusts a powerful few came together to monopolize whole industries, and in response populism spread like a prairie fire from farmers to factory workers. Silver or gold, tariff or free trade—the choices often seemed to be starkly opposed. The economy was similarly mercurial, a dichotomy of fabulous booms and enervating busts. Farmers expanded as rain watered the Plains like never before, then were driven off their land by drought. Invention engendered entrepreneurship and industry. The population became more urban.

The country's territory continued to get bigger, too, most notably with the massive addition of Alaska, But the United States also got metaphorically smaller, with previously isolated regions linked by the ever-expanding network of railroads. For Native Americans, their land became literally smaller. By the end of the century, even Oklahoma, which had waited at the end of the Trail of Tears for many Indians, was itself overrun with settlers. For most of the period cattle still roamed Western ranges, driven to rail depots in Kansas for delivery to meat-packing plants in Chicago. But as the railroads brought Americans west, ranchers fenced off the range. The frontier was disappearing.

In short, the United States had become a very big country facing very big changes. With the advent of 20th century, many more were yet to come.

CHINESE EXCLUSION ACT (1882)

Source: *The Public Statutes at Large of the United States of America from the Organization of the Government in 1789, etc., etc.*, Vol. XXII, pp. 58–61.

An act to execute certain treaty stipulations relating to Chinese

Whereas, in the opinion of the government of the United States the coming of Chinese laborers to this country endangers the good order of certain localities within the territory thereof; therefore,

Be it enacted by the Senate and House of Representatives of the United States of America in Congress assembled, that from and after the expiration of ninety days next after the passage of this act, and until the expiration of ten years next after the passage of this act, the coming of Chinese laborers to the United States be, and the same is hereby, suspended; and during such suspension it shall not be lawful for any Chinese laborer to come, or, having so come after the expiration of said ninety days, to remain within the United States.

Section 2. That the master of any vessel who shall knowingly bring within the United States on such vessel, and land or permit to be landed, any Chinese laborer from any foreign port or place shall be deemed guilty of a misdemeanor, and on conviction thereof shall be punished by a fine of not more than $500 for each and every such Chinese laborer so brought, and may be also imprisoned for a term not exceeding one year.

Section 3. That the two foregoing sections shall not apply to Chinese laborers who were in the United States on the 17th day of November, 1880, or who shall have come into the same before the expiration of ninety days next after the passage of this act, and who shall produce to such master before going on board such vessel, and shall produce to the collector of the port in the United States at which such vessel shall arrive, the evidence hereinafter in this act required of his being one of the laborers in this section mentioned; nor shall the two foregoing sections apply to the case of any master whose vessel, being bound to a port not within the United States, shall come within the jurisdiction of the United States by reason of being in distress or in stress of weather, or touching at any port of the United States on its voyage to any foreign port or place: Provided, that all Chinese laborers brought on such vessel shall depart with the vessel on leaving port....

Section 6. That in order to the faithful execution of Articles I and II of the treaty [of 1880]...every Chinese person other than a laborer who may be entitled by said treaty and this act to come within the United States, and who shall be about to come to the United States, shall be identified as so entitled by the Chinese government in each case, such identity to be evidenced by a certificate issued under the authority of said government, which certificate shall be in the English language or (if not in the English language) accompanied by a translation into English, stating such right to come, and which certificate shall state the name, title, or official rank, if any, the age, height, and all physical peculiarities, former and present occupation or profession, and place of residence in China of the person to whom the certificate is issued and that such person is entitled conformably to the treaty...to come within the United States. Such certificate shall be prima facie evidence of the fact set forth therein, and shall be produced to the collector of customs, or his deputy, of the port in the district in the United States at which the person named therein shall arrive....

Section 8. That the master of any vessel arriving in the United States from any foreign port or place shall...deliver and report to the collector of customs of the district in which such vessels shall have arrived a separate list of all Chinese passengers taken on board his vessel at any foreign port.... Any willful refusal or neglect of any such master to comply with the provisions of this section shall incur the same penalties and forfeiture as are provided for a refusal or neglect to report and deliver a manifest of the cargo....

Section 11. That any person who shall knowingly bring into or cause to be brought into the United States by land, or who shall knowingly aid or abet the same, or aid or abet the landing in the United States from any vessel of any Chinese person not lawfully entitled to enter the United States, shall be deemed guilty of a misdemeanor, and shall, on conviction thereof, be fined in a sum not exceeding $1,000, and imprisoned for a term not exceeding one year.

Section 12. That no Chinese person shall be permitted to enter the United States by land without producing to the proper officer of customs the certificate in this act required of Chinese persons seeking to land from a vessel. And any Chinese person found unlawfully within the United States shall be caused to be removed therefrom to the country from whence he came, by direction of the President of the United States, and at the cost of the United States, after being brought before some justice, judge, or commissioner of a court of the United States and found to be one not lawfully entitled to be or remain in the United States.

Section 13. That this act shall not apply to diplomatic and other officers of the Chinese government traveling upon the business of that government, whose credentials shall be taken as equivalent to the certificate in this act mentioned, and shall exempt them and their body and household servants from the provisions of this act as to other Chinese persons.

Section 14. That hereafter no state court or court of the United States shall admit Chinese to citizenship; and all laws in conflict with this act are hereby repealed.

Section 15. That the words "Chinese laborers" wherever used in this act shall be construed to mean both skilled and unskilled laborers and Chinese employed in mining.

WILLIAM H. SEWARD: THE PROMISE OF ALASKA (1869)

Source: *Old South Leaflets*, 133 (published by the Directors of the Old South Work, Old South Meeting House, Boston, n.d.).

Citizens of Alaska, Fellow Citizens of the United States:

You have pressed me to meet you in public assembly once before I leave Alaska. It would be sheer affectation to pretend to doubt your sincerity in making this request, and capriciously ungrateful to refuse it, after having received so many and varied hospitalities from all sorts and conditions of men. It is not an easy task, however, to speak in a manner worthy of your consideration while I am living constantly on shipboard, as you all know, and am occupied intently in searching out whatever is sublime, or beautiful, or peculiar, or useful.

On the other hand, it is altogether natural on your part to say, "You have looked upon Alaska; what do you think of it?" Unhappily, I have seen too little of Alaska to answer the question satisfactorily. The entire coastline of the United States, exclusive of Alaska, is 10,000 miles, while the coastline of Alaska alone, including the islands, is 26,000 miles. The portion of the territory which lies east of the peninsula, including islands, is 120 miles wide. The western portion, including Aleutian Islands, expands to a breadth of 2,200 miles. The entire land area, including islands, is 577,390 statute square miles.

We should think a foreigner very presumptuous who should presume to give the world an opinion of the whole of the United States of America after he had merely looked in from his steamer at Plymouth and Boston Harbor, or had run up the Hudson River to the Highlands, or had ascended the Delaware to Trenton, or the James River to Richmond, or the Mississippi no farther than Memphis. My observation thus far has hardly been more comprehensive.

I entered the Territory of Alaska at the Portland Canal, made my way through the narrow passages of the Prince of Wales Archipelago, thence through Peril and Chatham Straits and Lynn Channel, and up the Chilcat River to the base of Fairweather, from which latter place I have returned through Clarence Straits, to sojourn a few days in your beautiful bay, under the shadows of the Baranoff Hills and Mount Edgecombe....

Alaska has been as yet but imperfectly explored; but enough is known to assure us that it possesses treasures of what are called the baser ores equal to those of any other region of the continent. We have Copper Island and Copper

River, so named as the places where the natives, before the period of the Russian discovery, had procured the pure metal from which they fabricated instruments of war and legendary shields.

In regard to iron, the question seems to be not where it can be found but whether there is any place where it does not exist. Mr. Davidson of the Coast Survey invited me to go up to him at the station he had taken up the Chilcat River to make his observations of the eclipse, by writing me that he had discovered an iron mountain there. When I came there, I found that, very properly, he had been studying the heavens so busily that he had but cursorily examined the earth under his feet; that it was not a single iron mountain he had discovered but a range of hills the very dust of which adheres to the magnet; while the range itself, 2,000 feet high, extends along the east bank of the river thirty miles.

Limestone and marble crop out on the banks of the same river and in many other places. Coal beds, accessible to navigation, are found at Kootznoo. It is said, however, that the concentrated resin which the mineral contains renders it too inflammable to be safely used by steamers. In any case, it would seem calculated to supply the fuel requisite for the manufacture of iron. What seems to be excellent cannel coal is also found in the Prince of Wales Archipelago. There are also mines at Cook's Inlet. Placer and quartz gold mining is pursued under many social disadvantages upon the Stickeen and elsewhere, with a degree of success which, while it does not warrant us in assigning a superiority in that respect to the territory, does nevertheless warrant us in regarding gold mining as an established and reliable resource.

It would argue inexcusable insensibility if I should fail to speak of the scenery which, in the course of my voyage, has seemed to pass like a varied and magnificent panorama before me. The exhibition did not, indeed, open within the territory. It broke upon me first when I had passed Cape Flattery and entered the Straits of Fuca, which separate British Columbia from Washington Territory. It widened as I passed along the shore of Puget Sound, expanded in the waters which divide Vancouver from the continent, and finally spread itself out into a magnificent archipelago, stretching through the entire Gulf of Alaska and closing under the shade of Mounts Fairweather and St. Elias. Nature has furnished to this majestic picture the only suitable border which could be conceived by lifting the coast range mountains to an exalted height, and clothing them with eternal snows and crystalline glaciers.

It remains only to speak of man and of society in Alaska. Until the present moment the country has been exclusively inhabited and occupied by some thirty or more Indian tribes. I incline to doubt the popular classification of these tribes upon the assumption that they have descended from diverse races. Climate and other circumstances have indeed produced some differences of manners and customs between the Aleuts, the Koloschians, and the interior continental tribes. But all of them are manifestly of Mongol origin. Although they have preserved no common traditions, all alike indulge in tastes, wear a physiognomy, and are imbued with sentiments peculiarly noticed in Japan and China.

Savage communities, no less than civilized nations, require space for subsistence, whether they depend for it upon the land or upon the sea—in savage communities especially; and increase of population disproportioned to the supplies of the country occupied necessitates subdivision and remote colonization. Oppression and cruelty occur even more frequently among barbarians than among civilized men. Nor are ambition and faction less inherent in the one condition than in the other. From these causes it has happened that the 25,000 Indians in Alaska are found permanently divided into so many insignificant nations.

These nations are jealous, ambitious, and violent; could in no case exist long in the same region without mutually affording what, in every case, to each party seems just cause of war. War between savages becomes the private cause of the several families which are afflicted with the loss of their members. Such a war can never be composed until each family which has suffered receives an indemnity in blankets, adjusted according to an imaginary tariff, or, in the failure of such compensation, secures the death of one or more enemies as an atonement for the injury it has sustained. The enemy captured, whether by superior force or

strategy, either receives no quarter or submits for himself and his progeny to perpetual slavery.

It has thus happened that the Indian tribes of Alaska have never either confederated or formed permanent alliances, and that even at this late day, in the presence of superior power exercised by the United States government, they live in regard to each other in a state of enforced and doubtful truce. It is manifest that, under these circumstances, they must steadily decline in numbers; and, unhappily, this decline is accelerated by their borrowing ruinous vices from the white man.

Such as the natives of Alaska are, they are, nevertheless, in a practical sense, the only laborers at present in the territory. The white man comes among them from London, from St. Petersburg, from Boston, from New York, from San Francisco, and from Victoria, not to fish (if we except alone the whale fishery) or to hunt but simply to buy what fish and what peltries, ice, wood, lumber, and coal the Indians have secured under the superintendence of temporary agents or factors.

When we consider how greatly most of the tribes are reduced in numbers and how precarious their vocations are, we shall cease to regard them as indolent or incapable; and, on the contrary, we shall more deeply regret than ever before that a people so gifted by nature, so vigorous and energetic, and withal so docile and gentle in their intercourse with the white man, can neither be preserved as a distinct social community nor incorporated into our society. The Indian tribes will do here as they seem to have done in Washington Territory and British Columbia—they will merely serve their turn until civilized white men come.

You, the citizens of Sitka, are the pioneers, the advanced guard of the future population of Alaska; and you naturally ask when, from whence, and how soon reenforcements shall come, and what are the signs and guarantees of their coming. This question, with all its minute and searching interrogations, has been asked by the pioneers of every state and territory of which the American Union is now composed; and the history of those states and territories furnishes the complete, conclusive, and satisfactory answer. Emigrants go to every infant state and territory in obedience to the great natural law that obliges needy men to seek subsistence, and invites adventurous men to seek fortune where it is most easily obtained; and this is always in the new and uncultivated regions. They go from every state and territory, and from every foreign nation in America, Europe, and Asia, because no established and populous state or nation can guarantee subsistence and fortune to all who demand them among its inhabitants.

The guarantees and signs of their coming to Alaska are found in the resources of the territory, which I have attempted to describe, and in the condition of society in other parts of the world. Some men seek other climes for health and some for pleasure. Alaska invites the former class by a climate singularly salubrious and the latter class by scenery which surpasses in sublimity that of either the Alps, the Apennines, the Alleghenies, or the Rocky Mountains. Emigrants from our own states, from Europe, and from Asia will not be slow in finding out that fortunes are to be gained by pursuing here the occupations which have so successfully sustained races of untutored men.

Civilization and refinement are making more rapid advances in our day than at any former period. The rising states and nations on this continent, the European nations, and even those of eastern Asia, have exhausted, or are exhausting, their own forests and mines, and are soon to become largely dependent upon those of the Pacific. The entire region of Oregon, Washington Territory, British Columbia, and Alaska seem thus destined to become a shipyard for the supply of all nations.

I do not forget on this occasion that British Columbia belongs within a foreign jurisdiction. That circumstance does not materially affect my calculations. British Columbia, by whomsoever possessed, must be governed in conformity with the interests of her people and of society upon the American continent. If that territory shall be so governed, there will be no ground of complaint anywhere. If it shall be governed so as to conflict with the interests of the inhabitants of that territory and of the United States, we all can easily foresee what will happen in that case. You will ask me, however, for guarantees that the hopes I encourage will not be postponed. I give them.

Within the period of my own recollection, I have seen twenty new states added to the eighteen which before that time constituted the American Union; and I now see, besides Alaska, ten territories in a forward condition of preparation for entering into the same great political family. I have seen in my own time, not only the first electric telegraph but even the first railroad and the first steamboat invented by man. And even on this present voyage of mine, I have fallen in with the first steamboat, still afloat, that thirty-five years ago lighted her fires on the Pacific Ocean. These, citizens of Sitka, are the guarantees, not only that Alaska has a future, but that that future has already begun.

I know that you want two things just now, when European monopoly is broken down and United States free trade is being introduced within the territory: these are military protection while your number is so inferior to that of the Indians around you, and you need also a territorial civil government. Congress has already supplied the first of these wants adequately and effectually. I doubt not that it will supply the other want during the coming winter. It must do this because our political system rejects alike anarchy and executive absolutism. Nor do I doubt that the political society to be constituted here, first as a territory and ultimately as a state or many states will prove a worthy constituency of the republic.

To doubt that it will be intelligent, virtuous, prosperous, and enterprising is to doubt the experience of Scotland, Denmark, Sweden, Holland, and Belgium, and of New England and New York. Nor do I doubt that it will be forever true in its republican instincts and loyal to the American Union; for the inhabitants will be both mountaineers and seafaring men. I am not among those who apprehend infidelity to liberty and the Union in any quarter hereafter; but I am sure that, if constancy and loyalty are to fail anywhere, the failure will not be in the states which approach nearest to the North Pole.

Fellow citizens, accept once more my thanks, from the heart of my heart, for kindness which can never be forgotten, and suffer me to leave you with a sincere and earnest farewell.

HENRY ENO: SILVER IN NEVADA (1869)

Source: *Twenty Years on the Pacific Slope; Letters of Henry Eno from California and Nevada, 1848–1871.* W. Turrentine Jackson, ed., New Haven, 1965.

Dear Brother:

Yours of the 11th August was received yesterday. Have now been here since the 3rd of July. I came here expecting to find a rich mineral country, also to find much such a population as California had in 1849 and '50. The great mineral wealth of eastern Nevada has not been exaggerated. In fact I did not expect to find so rich or so many silver mines. There is not so much wild reckless extravagance among the people of the towns and the miners as in the early days of California. There are not as many homicides according to the numbers, but there is perhaps more highway robberies committed. We have here, as twenty years ago, numbers too lazy to work but not too lazy to steal, and some too proud to work and not afraid to steal. The laws of Nevada license gambling, and here at Hamilton, in Treasure City, and Shermantown are some ten or twelve licensed gambling tables. The next session of the legislature may perhaps license highway robbery.

There are two banking establishments, two express offices. Wells Fargo and Union Express, some ten or twelve assay offices, and a small army of lawyers. The District Court has been in session ever since I arrived. A trial often occupies ten or twelve days. A very few lawyers are doing well. From what I can discover I believe that lawyers depend more upon perjury and subornation of perjury than upon principles of law or precedents. Experts in mining do a thriving business as witnesses.

There are, I judge, nearly 200 paying mines within four miles square. There ought to be a dozen more quartz mills erected and would find full employment. The price of crushing and working ores is too high for low grade ores. The common price is $30 per ton. Under ordinary circumstances free ores yielding $15 per ton can be worked at a fair profit. There are very many mining districts within 80 and 100 miles that are now attracting attention of miners and capitalists. The merchants of Chicago are turning their attention to this silver country

and will enter into competition with San Francisco, and I should not be surprised if they succeed in establishing and building up a heavy business and a profitable one. The money market in California as well as in Nevada is very stringent. There is much financial distress. Very many men reputed to be worth their many thousands last spring are now reputed worthless. But in no country that I have ever seen (not even in California) do I believe that well-directed industry and judiciously invested capital would meet with richer rewards.

It will never be considered a good grain country, but as a pastoral country it is unquestionably a good one. Millions of sheep can be kept here and without cutting hay for winter. It is also a good dairy country. There is a great scarcity of water, it is true, but artesian wells can supply it. It is also a healthy country: no fever and ague. At this high elevation, persons of weak lungs are subject to pneumonia, but a little care will prevent it. It is no money, not pneumonia, that I am troubled about and am afraid it will become chronic.

I went out a few days ago with a young fellow on a prospecting trip, about four or five miles from here. Went over as rough a country as I ever traveled over. Stiping Mountain is but a molehill compared with ours. On our return, struck a silver lode. Brought home some specimens and had them assayed. Send you the assay, so that you may see how we manage here. Intend to prospect it further.

Have made up my mind to go to Iowa and St. Louis, if I can possibly raise the means, the forepart of October and return in the spring. I made the acquaintance of Judge G. C. Bates of Chicago who was here a short time since. I formerly knew him in Sacramento. He tells me I can make money by lecturing, advises me to make my debut at Chicago, and that he will introduce me. And also at Detroit. Am now busily engaged in preparing several lectures, but I labor under many disadvantages. Still hope to overcome them. If I can but put my foot on the lower round of fortune's ladder and grasp with my hand another, I have faith to believe I can yet climb it.

Was pleased to hear about your farming operations. Reapers, mowing machines, gang plows, and the thresh-ers have found their way to the Pacific Coast. Between Elko and Hamilton there are several mowing machines at work. Almost all the wheat of California is harvested by machines. Last year a Mr. Mitchell on the San Joaquin plains raised 14,000 acres of wheat, and this year Bidwell of the Sacramento Valley, candi-date for governor last year, raised 27,000 acres of wheat. Last year, in June, I was in San Francisco. A farmer living near Sacramento River told me that he had 1,500 acres of wheat which would yield, on an average, 30 bushels to the acre. He said he could harvest it, thrash it, put in sacks, and store it in a warehouse in San Francisco within a fortnight's time. There have been fifty-six harvesting machines employed this year on the Salinas Plains. I crossed them in 1850, and there was not a furrow turned.

Our markets here are well supplied with everything man wants to sustain life and some of the luxuries. Flour, $8 per hundredweight; beef and mutton, 15 to 20 cents per lb.; sugar, 3 lbs. for $1; bacon, 30 cents per lb.; apples, peaches, apricots, nectarines, and grapes from California in abundance, all about 25 cents per lb.; potatoes, 10 cents per lb.; beans the same; and water, 1212 cents a bucket; $7 a day for a horse to ride—I find it cheaper to go afoot—wood, $6 per cord. Rents all the way from $40 to $400 per month for one or two rooms. Plenty of good air but of rather a light quality, nothing.

I think you would like a trip to this wild country and to the more civilized portions of California. It would give materials for thought and reflection and would in all probability enable you to enjoy with a greater zest the comforts of a quiet home. As for me, I feel as if I had no country and no home, but try to make the best of it wherever I am.

CHIEF JOSEPH: THE DISILLUSIONED INDIAN (1879)

Source: *North American Review*, April 1879: "An Indian's Views of Indian Affairs."

During the hot days (July 1878) we received notice that we were to be moved farther away from our own country. We were not asked if we were willing to go. We were ordered to get into the railroad cars. Three of my people died on the way to Baxter Springs. It was worse to die there than to die fighting in the mountains.

We were moved from Baxter Springs (Kansas) to the Indian Territory, and set down without our lodges. We had but little medicine, and we were nearly all sick. Seventy of my people have died since we moved there.

We have had a great many visitors who have talked many ways. Some of the chiefs (General Fish and Colonel Stickney) from Washington came to see us, and selected land for us to live upon. We have not moved to that land, for it is not a good place to live.

The commissioner chief (E. A. Hayt) came to see us. I told him, as I told every one, that I expected General Miles's word would be carried out. He said it "could not be done; that white men now lived in my country and all the land was taken up; that, if I returned to Wallowa, I could not live in peace; that law-papers were out against my young men who began the war, and that the government could not protect my people." This talk fell like a heavy stone upon my heart. I saw that I could not gain anything by talking to him. Other law chiefs (congressional committee) came to see me and said they would help me to get a healthy country. I did not know who to believe. The white people have too many chiefs. They do not understand each other. They do not all talk alike.

The commissioner chief (Mr. Hayt) invited me to go with him and hunt for a better home than we have now. I like the land we found (west of the Osage reservation) better than any place I have seen in that country; but it is not a healthy land. There are no mountains and rivers. The water is warm. It is not a good country for stock. I do not believe my people can live there. I am afraid they will all die. The Indians who occupy that country are dying off. I promised Chief Hayt to go there, and do the best I could until the government got ready to make good General Miles's word. I was not satisfied, but I could not help myself.

Then the inspector chief (General McNiel) came to my camp and we had a long talk. He said I ought to have a home in the mountain country north, and that he would write a letter to the great chief at Washington. Again the hope of seeing the mountains of Idaho and Oregon grew up in my heart.

At last I was granted permission to come to Washington and bring my friend Yellow Bull and our interpreter with me. I am glad we came. I have shaken hands with a great many friends, but there are some things I want to know which no one seems to be able to explain. I can not understand how the government sends a man out to fight us, as it did General Miles, and then breaks his word. Such a government has something wrong about it. I can not understand why so many chiefs are allowed to talk so many different ways, and promise so many different things. I have seen the great father chief (the President), the next great chief (secretary of the interior), the commissioner chief (Hayt), the law chief (General Butler), and many other law chiefs (congressmen), and they all say they are my friends, and that I shall have justice, but while their mouths all talk right I do not understand why nothing is done for my people. I have heard talk and talk, but nothing is done. Good words do not last long unless they amount to something. Words do not pay for my dead people. They do not pay for my country, now overrun by white men. They do not protect my father's grave. They do not pay for all my horses and cattle. Good words will not give me back my children. Good words will not make good the promise of your war chief General Miles. Good words will not give my people good health and stop them from dying. Good words will not get my people a home where they can live in peace and take care of themselves. I am tired of talk that comes to nothing. It makes my heart sick when I remember all the good words and all the broken promises. There has been too much talking by men who had no right to talk. Too many misrepresentations have been made, too many misunderstandings have come up between the white men about the Indians. If the white man wants to live in peace with the Indian he can live in peace. There need be no trouble. Treat all men alike. Give them all the same law. Given them all an even chance to live and grow. All men were made by the same Great Spirit Chief. They are all brothers. The earth is the mother of all people, and all people should have equal rights upon it. You might as well expect the rivers to run backward as that any man who was born a free man should be contented when penned up and denied liberty to go where he pleases. If you tie a horse to a stake, do

you expect he will grow fat? If you pen an Indian up on a small spot of earth, and compel him to stay there, he will not be contented, nor will he grow and prosper. I have asked some of the great white chiefs where they get their authority to say to the Indian that he shall stay in one place, while he sees white men going where they please. They can not tell me.

I only ask of the government to be treated as all other men are treated. If I can not go to my own home, let me have a home in some country where my people will not die so fast. I would like to go to Bitter Root Valley. There my people would be healthy; where they are now they are dying. Three have died since I left my camp to come to Washington.

When I think of our condition my heart is heavy. I see men of my race treated as outlaws and driven from country to country, or shot down like animals.

I know that my race must change. We can not hold our own with the white men as we are. We only ask an even chance to live as other men live. We ask to be recognized as men. We ask that the same law shall work alike on all men. If the Indian breaks the law, punish him by the law. If the white man breaks the law, punish him also.

Let me be a free man—free to travel, free to stop, free to work, free to trade where I choose, free to choose my own teachers, free to follow the religion of my fathers, free to think and talk and act for myself—and I will obey every law, or submit to the penalty.

Whenever the white man treats the Indian as they treat each other, then we will have no more wars. We shall all be alike—brothers of one father and one mother, with one sky above us and one country around us, and one government for all. Then the Great Spirit Chief who rules above will smile upon this land, and send rain to wash out the bloody spots made by brothers' hands from the face of the earth. For this time the Indian race are waiting and praying. I hope that no more groans of wounded men and women will ever go to the ear of the Great Spirit Chief above, and that all people may be one people.

ANDREW CARNEGIE: THE PICTURE LOVER AND THE PICTURE BUYER (1886)

Source: *Triumphant Democracy*, Revised edition, New York, 1893, Ch. 11.

The world has long considered political rights and government the province of the few. So also has it considered art as beyond the multitude. In the political field the republic has proclaimed a new gospel, the right of every citizen to an equal share in the government. It is her mission also, we fully believe, to teach the nations that art should likewise be universal; not the luxury of the few but the heritage of the whole people. There are many proofs that good progress is now being made in this direction. The more general diffusion of art in every department is a marked and gratifying movement of our time. Art in the new land had naturally a feeble beginning.

In 1826 the National Academy of Design was organized in New York, under the presidency of Samuel F. B. Morse, as the successor of the American Academy of Fine Arts, which died after the fire of the same year had destroyed its art collection. Similar institutions had been founded early in Philadelphia and in Boston, but the National Academy has always exercised a paramount influence in the development of American art. It remains today the principal art society, although much in need of enlarged and better galleries situated farther uptown.

About ten years later the American Art Union, an incorporated institution for the distribution, by lot, of works of art, came into existence, and during more than a decade aided much in educating the people and in bringing into notice many artists who might otherwise have found it difficult to win recognition. But this gain was loss; the influence of the lottery system must have transcended a hundredfold any possible advantage gained through it by art. Happily, the day for such gambling is over, but we meet with the evil still where one would least expect it....

Several small public galleries, like those of the Athenaeum in Boston, and of the Historical Society in New York, and a few private collections were found in different parts of the country which exercised a considerable influence in raising the standard of popular taste. People began to buy pictures and, as was natural, began by buying very poor pictures. European dealers, taking advantage of the comparative ignorance of the country in art matters, flooded the principal cities with alleged examples of the old masters, which found a ready sale forty or fifty years ago, but which gradually disappeared as their worthlessness was understood; and now it would be difficult to find one of these early art treasures of America in any respectable house, unless it may have been preserved among the rubbish of the garret. The experience thus gained was of the utmost value.

The American, with his quick perception, soon learned to distinguish between the good and the bad, and though his taste may in some cases seem a little "loud" to the European connoisseur, he seldom buys anything which is absolutely worthless. He is recognized now in the European markets as one of the shrewdest as well as one of the most liberal buyers. Throughout the world, whenever art treasures come under the hammer, the American is found in competition with nobles, and even with crowned heads, and he is no mean competitor; for he is not afraid to spend his dollars where he is sure of getting his money's worth. Thus, during the past few decades, there has been a constant flow of works of art to the United States. There is no city of importance in the country which has not its public gallery of painting and sculpture, as well as many private collections in the houses of its citizens. These latter are often exhibited as loan collections and exert a most beneficial influence in creating a taste for art.

The movement of modern French paintings to this country began early in the seventies and was mainly due to the influence of William M. Hunt, of Boston, who had studied under Couture and Millet, and had become deeply impressed with the work that these artists and their great contemporaries were doing. He saw that these were landscapes and figures that were sure to live and to acquire more and more value as their superior qualities became better known. He returned to Boston full of enthusiasm over the Barbizon School, as it came to be called, taking its name from the little village on the edge of the Fontainebleau Forest where these artists—Millet, Rousseau, Diaz, Dupré, and others—had their studios. He imparted some of his enthusiasm to wealthy Boston amateurs, who began to import their paintings. New York was quick to appreciate their beauty, and soon the collectors of the two cities vied with each other in the attempt to secure choice examples of the work of these great painters and those associated with them, such as Corot, Daubigny, and Troyon.

From that time until now the New World has been steadily transferring to the galleries of its collectors the greatest paintings produced by this, the most famous school of artists of the century. The artists, the dealers, and the wealthy amateurs well knew the extent to which the best modern works of the French school were being imported to the private galleries of the United States. But the great public was hardly aware of the number and the value of these paintings until the Morgan and the Seney collections were thrown upon the market a few years ago. New York's private galleries, it was suddenly discovered, were filled with them, and the further fact was made manifest that the Shaw, Brimmer, Wigglesworth, and other Boston galleries contained some of the finest examples of the Barbizon School.

It is estimated by a good judge, who is thoroughly conversant with the private galleries, not only on the seaboard but in Detroit, Milwaukee, Cincinnati, Chicago, and other cities, that modern French art is better represented in the United States than it is in any country but France today. There are more than fifty examples of Meissonier alone in this country. And the eagerness of collectors to possess these great works, and their willingness to pay high prices for them, were well illustrated when Judge Hilton bought Meissonier's "1807" at the Stewart sale for $66,000. There is no doubt but that a loan collection of a hundred modern French paintings could be made in this country which could not be matched for quality or for commercial value anywhere else in the world, France alone excepted.

The lesson, my readers, of all this is not far to seek. It shows how the New is absorbing the art treasures of the Old World. When wealth and taste go hand in hand, such a movement, once begun, is bound to continue. Twenty-five years hence Frenchmen may have to visit the galleries of Boston, New York, Philadelphia, Pittsburgh, Baltimore, Cincinnati, Detroit, Chicago, and St. Paul in order to study the work of their own Fontainebleau School. None of these paintings return to France. When once here they are here for all time....

The foreign reader must not infer from what is said of the American fondness for the French school of art that the Americans have no painters of their own. They have hundreds of wonderfully clever painters who have mastered the technique, many having acquired their proficiency in the studios of the French masters. Sargent and Whistler are men whose genius is recognized in Paris and London as well as in America. Other names equally, or almost equally, famous, who, in the present generation, have won a high and enviable place, will occur to the reader. While we have not yet produced a Rousseau or a Daubigny, our group of landscape painters are doing admirable work—work that will live. In figure pictures and genre our painters are rapidly approaching the French. The average of our portrait painting is reputed to be as high as the English standard. If there is a branch in which American painters are weak, it is in the historical, allegorical, and imaginative. This was a field in which West and Allston excelled. The note of their time, however, was romantic, and they felt its influence and echoed it. The watchword of art at the present day is "truth to nature." By and by a reaction will set in, and the imagination will be given freer play.

Meanwhile much is being done to encourage American artists. The National Academy exhibitions have improved greatly in the last few years; the Society of American Artists exerts a stimulative influence; throughout the West, art is gaining the attention of the men who since the war have been bringing the continent into subjection; traveling scholarships and prizes have been generously established by which promising young men are sent abroad for a year's study; public galleries are becoming richer each year in works well worthy of attention; and in many other ways native art is being fostered. Several collections of paintings already prove what fine examples in every branch of art can be gathered among the works of native painters, if patience and taste and a patriotic pride in the achievements of one's fellow countrymen govern the selection. The gift of $1 million, netting $50,000 per annum, made to the Pittsburgh Art Gallery, is conditioned upon at least six pictures by American artists being purchased each successive year, to be displayed in chronological order. If the wishes of the donor be properly carried out by the Art Committee, we shall in time have a collection of great historical value as showing the development of the national school of painting.

The Fine Arts Society of New York deserves notice. In the whole history of artistic progress in the republic, we know of nothing to compare with this in several of its features. The Society is formed by a consolidation of the Architectural League, the Society of American Artists, and the Art Students' League. Each of these had a small fund and was able to contribute its third to a capital of $50,000. Upon this slender financial basis, but strong in faith and ability, the newly elected officers began their work, which in less than a year has culminated in the recent opening of the Fine Arts Building in Fifty-seventh Street, in which there have already been held three notable exhibitions, each among the best of its kind. The society is teaching 640 students. The total spent upon the property is less than $500,000, which causes every experienced visitor to inquire how so much could have been done with so little.

The secret is that it has been a labor of love throughout. The organizers and all the officers have labored without salary, the architect designed the building without compensation, and such a building as reflects credit upon Mr. Hardenbergh; the contractors worked without profit; and at the head of the whole matter was an irrepressible man whose name deserves to be recorded in the history of art progress in America. Knowing how greatly we shall incur his displeasure, we nevertheless venture to write it down in full — Howard Russell Butler. We know of no undertaking that shows the character of the American more thoroughly than this — such effort, enthusiasm, organizing power, general ability, and self-devotion. No wonder that such qualities attracted and held the attention and drew forth the support of our most important patrons of art. The new gallery, connected with the rear of the main building, is called the George W. Vanderbilt Gallery, and justly so, for he it was who surprised the society by conferring upon it this invaluable gift.

Would that my conscience would permit me to leave the subject of American painting without an expression of heartfelt regret that this new art society is far too much French — Frenchy. The recent exhibition, in the words of a true patron of art, "was almost as bad as the Salon — the subjects as a rule unworthy, the landscapes blurred and sketchy, and the nude vulgar." One consolation remains. These young Frenchy Americans are to be taught another needed lesson. The picture lover and the picture buyer, offended at such a display, will evince his displeasure by showing the value, or rather the no-value, he places upon works which attempt thus to prostitute art to vulgar and unholy ends. If art is to devote itself to the perpetuation of aught but what is noble and pure, may we never be cursed by possessing it. Thank the fates, American literature so far is pure.

America has developed within the past half-century a school of sculpture which has won recognition both at home and abroad, though a visit to the national capital and to the public squares of some of the larger cities would scarcely induce such an opinion. Many of her sculptors have been educated under Italian influences but have drawn their inspiration rather from the antique than the modern Italian school. Some who stand foremost at home today have not enjoyed the benefit, or disadvantage perhaps, of foreign instruction, and their works, consequently, possess more of the flavor of the soil, so to speak, than do those which have been executed in strict accordance with the academic rules transmitted from antiquity. It is possible that these may develop in time into a purely American school of sculpture, which shall be recognized and take its place as such in the art history of the world.

HENRY DEMAREST LLOYD: MONOPOLY AND SOCIAL CONTROL (1884)

Source: *North American Review*, June 1884.

When President Gowen of the Reading Railroad was defending that company, in 1875, before a committee of the Pennsylvania legislature, for having taken part in the combination of the coal companies to cure the evil of "too much coal" by putting up the price and cutting down the amount for sale, he pleaded that there were fifty trades in which the same thing was done. He had a list of them to show the committee. He said:

Every pound of rope we buy for our vessels or for our mines is bought at a price fixed by a committee of the rope manufacturers of the United States. Every keg of nails, every paper of tacks, all our screws and wrenches and hinges, the boiler flues for our locomotives are never bought except at the price fixed by the representatives of the mills that manufacture them. Iron beams for your houses or your bridges can be had only at the prices agreed upon by a combination of those who produce them. Fire brick, gas pipe, terracotta pipe for drainage, every keg of powder we buy to blast coal are purchased under the same arrangement. Every pane of window glass in this house was bought at a scale of prices established exactly in the same manner. White lead, galvanized sheet iron, hose and belting and files are bought and sold at a rate determined in the same way.

When my friend Mr. Lane was called upon to begin his speech the other day and wanted to delay because the stenographer had not arrived, I asked Mr. Collins, the stenographer of your committee, if he would not act. He said, no, it was against the rules of the committee of stenographers. I said, "Well, Mr. Collins, I will pay you anything you ask. I want to get off." "Oh," said he, "prices are established by our combination, and I cannot change them." And when we come to the cost of labor, which enters more than anything else in the cost of coal, we are met by a combination there and are often obliged to pay the price fixed by it.

Adam Smith said in 1776: "People of the same trade hardly meet together even for merriment and diversion but the conversation ends in a conspiracy against the public or in some contrivance to raise prices." The expansive ferment of the new industry, coming with the new science, the new land, and the new liberties of our era, broke up these "conspiracies," and for a century we have heard nothing of them; but the race to overrun is being succeeded by the struggle to divide, and combinations are reappearing on all sides. This anyone may see from the reports of the proceedings of the conventions and meetings of innumerable associations of manufacturers and dealers and even producers which are being held almost constantly. They all do something to raise prices or hold them up, and they wind up with banquets for which we pay.

Four years ago the Chicago Lumbermen's Exchange adopted a resolution declaring it to be "dishonorable" for any dealer to make lower prices than those published by it for the control of prices in one of the greatest lumber markets of the world. Monthly reports are required by this exchange from dealers so that accurate accounts may be kept of stock on hand in order to regulate prices. The price lists of the exchange are revised and made "honest" at monthly banquets. In February 1883, it was found that members who ostensibly adhered to the price lists dipped into the dishonorable practice of competition on the sly by giving buyers greater than the usual discounts. This was then forbidden, and another pathway of competition closed. ...

The mills of Puget Sound, which supply a large proportion of the lumber consumed in the Pacific states, formed a combination last year to regulate the production and sustain prices. It is said by the local newspapers that the mills which do not belong to the association are hired to stand idle, as there are too many mills, and the association finds it profitable to sustain prices at the cost of thousands of dollars paid out in this way. The lumber market of the Pacific Coast is ruled by the California Lumber Exchange, and that is controlled by a few powerful firms. The prices of redwood are fixed by the Redwood Manufacturers' Association, and those of pine by the Pine Manufacturers' Association. During the past year the retail dealers of San Francisco have had to sign contracts with these associations, binding themselves to buy only from members of the associations, to buy and sell only at prices fixed by them, to give time and discount only according to rule, and to keep accounts so that every item will be clear to the inspectors hired by the associations to look after the retailers. Finally, the retailer binds himself, if he is "found guilty" of committing any of the forbidden sins, to pay a fine which may amount to $1,000, to be divided among the faithful. The literature of business can show no more remarkable productions than the printed forms of these contracts. This system is in imitation of the "special contracts" with shippers which have been put in force by the Central Pacific Railroad.

Western ranchmen complain that the competition of buyers is disappearing. They declare that there exist at the Chicago stockyards combinations of buyers who, by their ability to make large purchases and their agreement to offer but one price, get cattle at their own figures. One member of the "ring" does the buying today; another tomorrow; and so on. The cattle kings have combinations to defend themselves from cattle thieves, state legislatures, and other enemies, and propose to extend this category so as to include the middlemen at the stockyards. The Stockgrowers' Association of Wyoming have $100 million in cattle. At the recent convention held by this body in Cheyenne, it was unanimously declared that its business had been "seriously injured by the pooling arrangements prevailing among buyers at the Chicago stockyards," and the executive committee were instructed to obtain the fullest possible information as to the means by which cattle might be shipped direct to the European consumer.

Last July, Messrs. Vanderbilt, Sloan, and one or two others out of several hundred owners of coal lands and coal railroads, met in the pleasant shadows of Saratoga to make "a binding arrangement for the control of the coal trade." "Binding arrangement" the sensitive coal presidents say they prefer to the word "combination." The gratuitous warmth of summer suggested to these men the need the public would have of artificial heat, at artificial prices, the coming winter. It was agreed to fix prices and to prevent the production of too much of the raw material of warmth by suspensions of mining. In anticipation of the arrival of the cold wave from Manitoba, a cold wave was sent out all over the United States, from their parlors in New York, in an order for half-time work by the miners during the first three months of this year, and for an increase of prices. These are the means this combination uses to keep down wages—the price of men, and keep up the price of coal—the wages of capital....

The coal combination was again investigated by the New York legislature in 1878, after the combination had raised the prices of coal in New York to double what they had been. The legislature found that private mine operators who were not burdened like the great companies with extravagant and often corrupt purchases of coal lands, heavily watered stock, and disadvantageous contracts forced on them by interested directors, and who have only to pay the actual cost of producing the coal, "can afford to sell at a much less price than the railroad coal-producing companies, and would do so if they could get transportation from the mines to the market." This is denied them by the great companies.

"The private operators," says the report, "either find themselves entirely excluded from the benefits of transportation by reason of the high freights, or find it for their interest to make contracts with the railroads by which they will not sell to others, and so the railroads have and will keep the control of the supply of the private operators." To those who will not make such contracts, rates are fixed excluding them from the market, with the result, usually, of forcing them to sell their property to the lords of the pool. "The combination," the committee declared,

"can limit the supply and thereby create such a demand and price as they may deem advisable." ...

One of the sights which this coal side of our civilization has to show is the presence of herds of little children of all ages, from six years upward, at work in the coal breakers, toiling in dirt and air thick with carbon dust, from dawn to dark, of every day in the week except Sunday. These coal breakers are the only schools they know. A letter from the coal regions in the *Philadelphia Press* declares that "there are no schools in the world where more evil is learned or more innocence destroyed than in the breakers. It is shocking to watch the vile practices indulged in by these children, to hear the frightful oaths they use, to see their total disregard for religion and humanity." In the upper part of Luzerne County, out of 22,000 inhabitants, 3,000 are children between six and fifteen years of age, at work in this way.

"There is always a restlessness among the miners," an officer of one of the New York companies said, "when we are working them on half time." The latest news from the region of the coal combination is that the miners are so dissatisfied with the condition in which they are kept, by the suspension of work and the importation of competing Hungarian laborers in droves, that they are forming a combination of their own, a revival of the old Miners and Laborers' Association, which was broken up by the labor troubles of 1874 and 1875.

Combination is busy in those soft-coal districts, whose production is so large that it must be sent to competitive markets. A pool has just been formed covering the annual product of 6 million tons of the mines of Ohio. Indiana and Illinois are to be brought in, and it is planned to extend it to all the bituminous-coal districts that compete with each other. The appearance of Mr. Vanderbilt, last December, in the Clearfield district of Pennsylvania, at the head of a company capitalized for $5 million, was the first entry of a metropolitan mind into this field. Mr. Vanderbilt's role is to be that of producer, carrier, dealer, and consumer, all in one.

Until he came, the district was occupied by a number of small companies and small operators, as used to be the case in the anthracite field in the old days. But the man who works himself, with his sons, in a small mine, cutting perhaps from twenty to forty tons a day, cannot expect to survive the approach of the Manhattan capitalist. The small Clearfield producers, looking at the fate of their kind in the anthracite country, greeted Mr. Vanderbilt's arrival with the question, "What is to become of us?" "If the small operator," said one of the great man's lieutenants, "goes to the wall, that is his misfortune, not our fault." In March last the prominent Clearfield companies gave notice that wages must be reduced on the 1st of April, and immediately thereafter a union of their employees resolved that if the reduction, which they declared to be "without reason," was made they would strike....

On the theory of "too much of everything," our industries, from railroads to workingmen, are being organized to prevent milk, nails, lumber, freights, labor, soothing syrup, and all these other things from becoming too cheap. The majority have never yet been able to buy enough of anything. The minority have too much of everything to sell. Seeds of social trouble germinate fast in such conditions. Society is letting these combinations become institutions without compelling them to adjust their charges to the cost of production, which used to be the universal rule of price. Our laws and commissions to regulate the railroads are but toddling steps in a path in which we need to walk like men. The change from competition to combination is nothing less than one of those revolutions which march through history with giant strides. It is not likely that this revolution will go backward. Nothing goes backward in this country except reform. When Stephenson said of railroads that where combination was possible competition was impossible, he was unconsciously declaring the law of all industry.

Man, the only animal which forgets, has already in a century or two forgotten that the freedom, the independence of his group, of the state, and even of the family, which he has enjoyed for a brief interval, have been unknown in most of the history of our race and in all the history of most races. The livery companies of London, with their gloomy guildhalls, their wealth, their gluttony and winebibbing, their wretched Irish estates, exist today, vain reminders to us of a time when the entire industry of Europe was regimented into organizations, voluntary at first, afterward adopted by the law, which did what our pools of railroads, laborers, manufacturers, and others are trying to do. Not only prices but manners were pooled. "The notion," says Cliffe Leslie, "that every man had a right to settle where he liked, to carry on any occupation he thought fit, and in whatever manner he chose, to demand the highest price he could get, or, on the contrary, to offer lower terms than anyone else, to make the largest profit possible, and to compete with other traders without restraint was absolutely contrary to the spirit of the ages that preceded ours." This system existed for centuries. It is so unlike our own that the contemplation of it may well shake us out of our conceit that the transitions, displacements, changes, upheavals, struggles, exterminations—from Indians to sewing women—of the last 250 years were the normal condition of the race.

Those were not exceptional times. Our day of free competition and free contract has been the exceptional era in history. Explorer, pioneer, protestant, reformer, captain of industry could not move in the harness of the guild brother, the vassal, the monk, and were allowed to throw away medieval uniforms. But now "the individual withers; the world is more and more." Society, having let the individual overrun the new worlds to be conquered, is reestablishing its lines of communication with him. Literary theorists still repeat the cant of individualism in law, politics, and morals; but the world

of affairs is gladly accepting, in lieu of the liberty of each to do as he will with his own, all it can get of the liberty given by laws that let no one do as he might with his own. The dream of the French Revolution, that man was good enough to be emancipated from the bonds of association and government by the simple proclamation of "Liberty, Fraternity and Equality," was but the frenzied expression of what was called freedom of self-interest in a quieter but not less bloody revolution, if the mortality of the factories, the mines, and the tenements be charged to its account. A rope cannot be made of sand; a society cannot be made of competitive units.

We have given competition its own way and have found that we are not good enough or wise enough to be trusted with this power of ruining ourselves in the attempt to ruin others. Free competition could be let run only in a community where everyone had learned to say and act, "I am the state." We have had an era of material inventions. We now need a renaissance of moral inventions, contrivances to tap the vast currents of moral magnetism flowing uncaught over the face of society. Morals and values rise and fall together. If our combinations have no morals, they can have no values. If the tendency to combination is irresistible, control of it is imperative.

Monopoly and antimonopoly, odious as these words have become to the literary ear, represent the two great tendencies of our time: monopoly, the tendency to combination; antimonopoly, the demand for social control of it. As the man is bent toward business or patriotism, he will negotiate combinations or agitate for laws to regulate them. The first is capitalistic; the second is social. The first, industrial; the second, moral. The first promotes wealth; the second, citizenship. These combinations are not to be waved away as fresh pictures of folly or total depravity. There is something in them deeper than that.

The Aryan has proved by the experience of thousands of years that he can travel. "But travel," Emerson says, "is the fool's paradise." We must now prove that we can stay at home and stand it as well as the Chinese have done. Future Puritans cannot emigrate from Southampton to Plymouth Rock. They can only sail from righteousness to righteousness. Our young men can no longer go west; they must go up or down. Not new land but new virtue must be the outlet for the future. Our halt at the shores of the Pacific is a much more serious affair than that which brought our ancestors to a pause before the barriers of the Atlantic and compelled them to practise living together for a few hundred years. We cannot hereafter, as in the past, recover freedom by going to the prairies; we must find it in the society of the good.

In the presence of great combinations, in all departments of life, the moralist and patriot have work to do of a significance never before approached during the itinerant phases of our civilization. It may be that the coming age of combination will issue in a nobler and fuller liberty for the individual than has yet been seen; but that consummation will be possible, not in a day of competitive trade but in one of competitive morals.

THE KNIGHTS OF LABOR (1878)

Source: Terence V. Powderly, *Thirty Years of Labor, 1859 to 1889*, Columbus, Ohio, 1889, pp. 243–245.

- To bring within the folds of organization every department of productive industry, making knowledge a standpoint for action and industrial and moral worth, not wealth, the true standard of individual and national greatness.
- To secure to the toilers a proper share of the wealth that they create; more of the leisure that rightfully belongs to them; more societary advantages; more of the benefits, privileges, and emoluments of the world; in a word, all those rights and privileges necessary to make them capable of enjoying, appreciating, defending, and perpetuating the blessings of good government.
- To arrive at the true condition of the producing masses in their educational, moral, and financial condition by demanding from the various governments the establishment of Bureaus of Labor Statistics.
- The establishment of cooperative institutions, productive and distributive.

- The reserving of the public lands— the heritage of the people—for the actual settler—not another acre for railroads or speculators.
- The abrogation of all laws that do not bear equally upon capital and labor; the removal of unjust technicalities, delays, and discriminations in the administration of justice; and the adopting of measures providing for the health and safety of those engaged in mining, manufacturing, or building pursuits.
- The enactment of laws to compel chartered corporations to pay their employees weekly, in full, for labor performed during the preceding week, in the lawful money of the country.
- The enactment of laws giving mechanics and laborers a first lien on their work for their full wages.
- The abolishment of the contract system on national, state, and municipal work.
- The substitution of arbitration for strikes, whenever and wherever employers and employees are willing to meet on equitable grounds.
- The prohibition of the employment of children in workshops, mines, and factories before attaining their fourteenth year.
- To abolish the system of letting out by contract the labor of convicts in our prisons and reformatory institutions.

- To secure for both sexes equal pay for equal work.
- The reduction of the hours of labor to eight per day, so that the laborers may have more time for social enjoyment and intellectual improvement and be enabled to reap the advantages conferred by the labor-saving machinery which their brains have created.
- To prevail upon governments to establish a purely national circulating medium, based upon the faith and resources of the nation and issued directly to the people, without the intervention of any system of banking corporations, which money shall be a legal tender in payment of all debts, public or private.

THE PULLMAN STRIKE AND BOYCOTT (1894)

Source: 53 Congress, 3 Session, Senate Document No. 7, pp. 87–91, 578–581.

I. STATEMENT OF THE STRIKERS

Mr. President and brothers of the American Railway Union: We struck at Pullman because we were without hope. We joined the American Railway Union because it gave us a glimmer of hope. Twenty thousand souls, men, women, and little ones, have their eyes turned toward this convention today, straining eagerly through dark despondency for a glimmer of the heaven-sent message you alone can give us on this earth.

In stating to this body our grievances, it is hard to tell where to begin. You all must know that the proximate cause of our strike was the discharge of two members of our Grievance Committee the day after George M. Pullman, himself, and Thomas H. Wickes, his second vice-president, had guaranteed them absolute immunity. The more remote causes are still imminent. Five reductions in wages, in work, and in conditions of employment swept through the shops at Pullman between May and December 1893. The last was the most severe, amounting to nearly 30 percent, and our rents had not fallen. We owed Pullman $70,000 when we struck May 11. We owe him twice as much today. He does not evict us for two reasons: one, the force of popular sentiment and public opinion; the other, because he hopes to starve us out, to break through in the back of the American Railway Union, and to deduct from our miserable wages when we are forced to return to him the last dollar we owe him for the occupancy of his houses.

Rents all over the city in every quarter of its vast extent have fallen, in some cases to one-half. Residences, compared with which ours are hovels, can be had a few miles away at the prices we have been contributing to make a millionaire a billionaire. What we pay $15 for in Pullman is leased for $8 in Roseland; and remember that just as no man or woman of our 4,000 toilers has ever felt the friendly pressure of George M. Pullman's hand, so no man or woman of us all has ever owned or can ever hope to own one inch of George M. Pullman's land. Why, even the very streets are his. His ground has never been platted of record, and today he may debar any man who has acquiring rights as his tenant from walking in his highways. And those streets; do you know what he has named them? He says after the four great inventors in methods of transportation. And do you know what their names are? Why, Fulton, Stephenson, Watt, and Pullman.

Water which Pullman buys from the city at 8 cents a thousand gallons he retails to us at 500 percent advance and claims he is losing $400 a month on it. Gas which sells at 75 cents per thousand feet in Hyde Park, just north of us, he sells for $2.25. When we went to tell him our grievances, he said we were all his "children."

Pullman, both the man and the town, is an ulcer on the body politic. He owns the houses, the schoolhouses, and churches of God in the town he gave his once humble name. The revenue he derives from these, the wages he pays out with one hand—the Pullman Palace Car Company—he takes back with the other—the Pullman Land Association. He is able by this to bid under any contract car shop in this country. His competitors in business, to meet this, must reduce the wages of their men. This gives him the excuse to reduce ours to conform to the market. His business rivals must in turn scale down; so must he. And thus the merry war—the dance of skeletons bathed in human tears—goes on; and it will go on, brothers, forever unless you, the American Railway Union, stop it; end it; crush it out.

Our town is beautiful. In all these thirteen years no word of scandal has arisen against one of our women, young or old. What city of 20,000 persons can show the like? Since our strike, the arrests, which used to average four or five a day, had dwindled down to less than one a week. We are peaceable; we are orderly; and but for the kindly beneficence of kindly hearted people in and about Chicago we would be starving. We are not desperate today because we are not hungry, and our wives and children are not begging for bread. But George M. Pullman, who ran away from the public opinion that has arisen against him, like the genii from the bottle in the Arabian Nights, is not feeding us. He is patiently seated beside his millions waiting for what? To see us starve.

We have grown better acquainted with the American Railway Union these convention days, and as we have heard sentiments of the noblest philanthropy fall from the lips of our general officers— your officers and ours—we have learned that there is a balm for all our troubles, and that the box containing it is in your hands today, only awaiting opening to disseminate its sweet savor of hope.

George M. Pullman, you know, has cut our wages from 30 to 70 percent. George M. Pullman has caused to be paid in the last year the regular quarterly dividend of 2 percent on his stock and an extra slice of 112 percent, making 912 percent on $30

million of capital. George M. Pullman, you know, took three contracts on which he lost less than $5,000. Because he loved us? No. Because it was cheaper to lose a little money in his freight car and his coach shops than to let his workingmen go, but that petty loss, more than made up by us from money we needed to clothe our wives and little ones, was his excuse for effecting a gigantic reduction of wages in every department of his great works, of cutting men and boys and girls with equal zeal, including everyone in the repair shops of the Pullman Palace cars on which such preposterous profits have been made.

George M. Pullman will tell you, if you could go to him today, that he was paying better wages than any other car shops in the land. George M. Pullman might better save his breath. We have worked too often beside graduates from other establishments not to know that, work for work and skill for skill, no one can compete with us at wages paid for work well done. If his wage list showed a trifle higher, our efficiency still left us heavily the loser. He does not figure on our brain and muscle. He makes his paltry computation in dollars and cents.

We will make you proud of us, brothers, if you will give us the hand we need. Help us make our country better and more wholesome. Pull us out of our slough of despond. Teach arrogant grinders of the faces of the poor that there is still a God in Israel, and if need be a Jehovah—a God of battles. Do this, and on that last great day you will stand, as we hope to stand, before the great white throne "like gentlemen unafraid."

II. STATEMENT OF THE COMPANY

In view of the proposed attempt of the American Railway Union to interfere with public travel on railway lines using Pullman cars, in consequence of a controversy as to the wages of employees of the manufacturing department of the company, the Pullman Company requests the publication of the following statement of the facts, in face of which the attempt is to be made.

In the first week of May last, there were employed in the car manufacturing department at Pullman, Ill., about 3,100 persons. On May 7, a committee of the workmen had an interview by arrangement with Mr. Wickes, vice-president, at which the principal subject of discussion related to wages, but minor grievances as to shop administration were also presented, and it was agreed that another meeting should be held on the 9th of May, at which all the grievances should be presented in writing. The second meeting was held. As to the complaints on all matters except wages, it was arranged that a formal and thorough investigation should be made by Mr. Wickes, to be begun the next day, and full redress was assured to the committee as to all complaints proved to be well founded.

The absolute necessity of the last reduction in wages, under the existing condition of the business of car manufacturing, had been explained to the committee, and they were insisting upon a restoration of the wage scale of the first half of 1893, when Mr. Pullman entered the room and addressed the committee, speaking in substance as follows:

"At the commencement of the very serious depression last year, we were employing at Pullman 5,816 men and paying out in wages there $305,000 a month. Negotiations with intending purchasers of railway equipment that were then pending for new work were stopped by them, orders already given by others were canceled, and we were obliged to lay off, as you are aware, a large number of men in every department; so that by November 1, 1893, there were only about 2,000 men in all departments, or about one-third of the normal number. I realized the necessity for the most strenuous exertions to procure work immediately, without which there would be great embarrassment, not only to the employees and their families at Pullman but also to those living in the immediate vicinity, including between 700 and 800 employees who had purchased homes and to whom employment was actually necessary to enable them to complete their payments.

"I canvassed the matter thoroughly with the manager of the works and instructed him to cause the men to be assured that the company would do everything in its power to meet the competition which was sure to occur because of the great number of large car manufacturers that were in the same condition and that were exceedingly anxious to keep their men employed. I knew that if there was any work to be let, bids for it would be made upon a much lower basis than ever before.

"The result of this discussion was a revision in piecework prices, which, in the absence of any information to the contrary, I supposed to be acceptable to the men under the circumstances. Under these conditions, and with lower prices upon all materials, I personally undertook the work of the lettings of cars, and, by making lower bids than other manufacturers, I secured work enough to gradually increase our force from 2,000 up to about 4,200, the number employed, according to the April payrolls, in all capacities at Pullman.

"This result has not been accomplished merely by reduction in wages, but the company has borne its full share by eliminating from its estimates the use of capital and machinery, and in many cases going even below that and taking work at considerable loss, notably the 55 Long Island cars, which was the first large order of passenger cars let since the great depression and which was sought for by practically all the leading car builders in the country. My anxiety to secure that order so as to put as many men at work as possible was such that I put in a bid at more than $300 per car less than the actual cost to the company. The 300 stock cars built for the Northwestern Road and the 250 refrigerator cars now under construction for the same company will result in a loss of at least $12 per car, and the 25 cars just built for the Lake Street elevated road show a loss of $79 per car. I mention these particulars so that

you may understand what the company has done for the mutual interests and to secure for the people at Pullman and vicinity the benefit of the disbursement of the large sums of money involved in these and similar contracts, which can be kept up only by the procurement of new orders for cars; for, as you know, about three-fourths of the men must depend upon contract work for employment.

"I can only assure you that if this company now restores the wages of the first half of 1893, as you have asked, it would be a most unfortunate thing for the men because there is less than sixty days of contract work in sight in the shops under all orders, and there is absolutely no possibility, in the present condition of affairs throughout the country, of getting any more orders for work at prices measured by the wages of May 1893. Under such a scale the works would necessarily close down and the great majority of the employees be put in idleness, a contingency I am using my best efforts to avoid.

"To further benefit the people of Pullman and vicinity, we concentrated all the work that we could command at that point by closing our Detroit shops entirely and laying off a large number of men at our other repair shops, and gave to Pullman the repair of all cars that could be taken care of there.

"Also, for the further benefit of our people at Pullman, we have carried on a large system of internal improvements, having expended nearly $160,000 since August last in work which, under normal conditions, would have been spread over one or two years. The policy would be to continue this class of work to as great an extent as possible, provided, of course, the Pullman men show a proper appreciation of the situation by doing whatever they can to help themselves to tide over the hard times which are so seriously felt in every part of the country.

"There has been some complaint made about rents. As to this I would say that the return to this company on the capital invested in the Pullman tenements for the last year and the year before was 3.82 percent. There are hundreds of tenements in Pullman renting from $6 to $9 per month, and the tenants are relieved from the usual expenses of exterior cleaning and the removal of garbage, which is done by the company. The average amount collected from employees for gas consumed is about $2 a month. To ascertain the exact amount of water used by tenants, separate from the amount consumed by the works, we have recently put in meters, by which we find that the water consumed by the tenants, if paid for at the rate of 4 cents per 1,000 gallons, in accordance with our original contract with the village of Hyde Park, would amount to about $1,000 a month, almost exactly the rate which we have charged the tenants, this company assuming the expense of pumping. At the increased rate the city is now charging us for water, we are paying about $500 a month in excess of the amount charged to the tenants. The present payrolls at Pullman amount to about $7,000 a day."

On the question of rents, while, as stated above, they make a manifestly inadequate return upon the investment, so that it is clear they are not, in fact, at an arbitrarily high figure, it may be added that it would not be possible in a business sense so to deal with them.

The renting of the dwellings and the employment of workmen at Pullman are in no way tied together. The dwellings and apartments are offered for rent in competition with those of the immediately adjacent towns of Kensington, Roseland, and Gano. They are let alike to Pullman employees and to very many others in no way connected with the company, and, on the other hand, many Pullman employees rent or own their homes in those adjacent towns. The average rental at Pullman is at the rate of $3 per room per month. There are 1,200 tenements, of varying numbers of rooms, the average monthly rental of which is $10; of these there are 600 the average monthly rental of which is $8. In very many cases, men with families pay a rent seemingly large for a workman, but which is in fact reduced in part, and often wholly repaid, by the subrents paid by single men as lodgers.

On May 10, the day after the second conference above mentioned, work went on at Pullman as usual, and the only incident of note was the beginning by Mr. Wickes, assisted by Mr. Brown, the general manager of the company, of the promised formal investigation at Pullman of the shop complaints.

A large meeting of employees had been held the night before at Kensington, which, as was understood by the company, accepted the necessity of the situation preventing an increase of wages; but at a meeting of the local committee held during the night of May 10, a strike was decided upon, and, accordingly, the next day about 2,500 of the employees quit their work, leaving about 600 at work, of whom very few were skilled workmen. As it was found impracticable to keep the shops in operation with a force thus diminished and disorganized, the next day those remaining were necessarily laid off, and no work has since been done in the shops.

The payrolls at the time amounted to about $7,000 a day and were reduced $5,500 by the strike, so that during the period of a little more than six weeks which has elapsed the employees who quit their work have deprived themselves and their comrades of earnings of more than $200,000.

It is an element of the whole situation worthy of note that at the beginning of the strike the Pullman Savings Bank had on deposit in its savings department $488,000, of which about nine-tenths belonged to employees at Pullman, and that this amount has since been reduced by the sum of $32,000.

While deploring the possibility of annoyance to the public by the threats of irresponsible organizations to interrupt the orderly ministration to the comfort of travelers on railway lines, aggregating 125,000 miles in length, the Pullman Company can do no more than explain its situation to the public.

It has two separate branches of business, essentially distinct from each other. One is to provide sleeping cars, which are delivered by it under contract to the various railway companies, to be run by them on their lines as a part of their trains for the carriage of their passengers, over the movements of which this company has no control. Contract arrangements provide for the making of all repairs to such cars by the railway companies using them—as to certain repairs absolutely and as to all others upon the request of the Pullman Company, which ordinarily finds it most convenient to use its own manufacturing facilities to make such repairs. The other, and a distinct branch of the business of the Pullman Company, is the manufacture of sleeping cars for the above-mentioned use of railway companies and the manufacture for sale to railway companies of freight cars and ordinary passenger cars, and of streetcars, and this business is almost at a standstill throughout the United States.

The business of manufacturing cars for sale gives employment to about 70 percent of the shop employees. The manufacture of sleeping cars for use by railway companies under contract, and which, under normal conditions, gives employment to about 15 percent of the shop employees, cannot be resumed by the company to an important extent for a very long time; for, out of the provision made for the abnormal travel last year, the company now has about 400 sleeping cars in store ready for use, but for which there is no need in the existing conditions of public travel.

It is now threatened by the American Railway Union officials that railway companies using Pullman sleeping cars shall be compelled to deprive their passengers of sleeping-car accommodations unless the Pullman Company will agree to submit to arbitration the question as to whether or not it shall open its manufacturing shops at Pullman and operate them under a scale of wages which would cause a daily loss to it of one-fourth the wages paid.

SAMUEL GOMPERS: THE LABORER'S RIGHT TO LIFE (1894)

Source: *American Federationist*, September 1894.

Dear Sir:

I have the honor to acknowledge the receipt of your favor of the 31st ult., the contents of which I have carefully noted. Possibly I should have written you earlier, but more important matters demanded my immediate consideration. I hope, however, that you have suffered no inconvenience or pain of injustice done you by reason of this delay.

You say that I have misquoted you in my article in the *North American Review* in attributing to you the following words in your Decoration Day address at Galesburg: "The growth of labor organizations must be restrained by law." Upon closer examination you will find that I did not use the word "restrained,"

but "checked." However, this makes little material difference, except to show that unintentionally one man may misquote another.

The words I quoted I saw in several newspaper accounts of your address, and I am exceedingly pleased that you favor me with a printed copy of it, which I have read with much interest. In perusing that address I find that you said (page 12): "Restore to each individual by the enforcement of law, not simply his right but if possible a returning sense of duty to control his own personality and property. Let us set a limit to the field of organization."

Of course this citation from the printed address you send me does not contain the words I attributed to you, but you say in your letter that I will not find either that you used the words or that you "expressed that sentiment." To my untutored mind there may not be that grave difference which your legal learning can discern in limiting by law the field of organization and checking its growth by law.

I doubt that the thinking world will hold me chargeable of having done you a grave injustice, and I feel convinced after a perusal of your address that both in fact and in spirit you gave utterance to the sentiment I attribute to you, and which you either fail to remember or regret.

You say that, as you stated in your charge to the grand jury, you believe in labor organizations within such lawful and reasonable limits as will make them a service to the laboring man and not a menace to the lawful institutions of the country. I have had the pleasure of reading your charge to the grand jury, and have only partially been able to discover how far you believe in labor organizations.

You would certainly have no objection officially or personally to workingmen organizing, and in their meetings discuss perhaps "the origin of man," benignly smiling upon each other and declaring that all existing things are right, going to their wretched homes to find some freedom in sleep from gnawing hunger. You would have them extol the virtues of monopolists and wreckers of the people's welfare. You would not have them consider seriously the fact that more than 2 million of their fellows are unemployed, and though willing and able, cannot find the opportunity to work in order that they may sustain themselves, their wives, and their children. You would not have them consider seriously the fact that Pullman who has grown so rich from the toil of his workmen that he can riot in luxury, while he heartlessly turns these very workmen out of their tenements into the streets and leave to the tender mercies of corporate greed. Nor would you have them ponder upon the hundreds of other Pullmans of different names.

You know, or ought to know, that the introduction of machinery is turning into idleness thousands faster than new industries are founded, and yet, machinery certainly should not be either destroyed or hampered in its full development. The laborer is a man, he is made warm by the same sun and made cold—yes, colder —by the same winter as you are. He has a heart and brain, and feels and knows the human and paternal instinct for those depending upon him as keenly as do you.

What shall the workers do? Sit idly by and see the vast resources of nature and the human mind be utilized and monopolized for the benefit of the comparative few? No. The laborers must learn to think and act, and soon, too, that only by the power of organization and common concert of action can either their manhood be maintained, their rights to life (work to sustain it) be recognized, and liberty and rights secured.

Since you say that you favor labor organizations within certain limits, will you kindly give to thousands of your anxious fellow citizens what you believe the workers could and should do in their organizations to solve this great problem? Not what they should not do. You have told us that.

I am not one of those who regards the entire past as a failure. I recognize the progress made and the improved conditions of which nearly the entire civilized world are the beneficiaries. I ask you to explain, however, that if the wealth of the whole world is, as you say, "preeminently and beneficially the nation's wealth," how is it that thousands of able-bodied, willing, earnest men and women are suffering the pangs of hunger? We may boast of our wealth and civilization, but to the hungry man and woman and child our progress is a hollow mockery, our civilization a sham, and our "national wealth" a chimera.

You recognize that the industrial forces set in motion by steam and electricity have materially changed the structure of our civilization. You also admit that a system has grown up where the accumulations of the individual have passed from his control into that of representative combinations and trusts, and that the tendency in this direction is on the increase. How, then, can you consistently criticize the workingmen for recognizing that as individuals they can have no influence in deciding what the wages, hours of toil, and conditions of employment shall be?

You evidently have observed the growth of corporate wealth and influence. You recognize that wealth, in order to become more highly productive, is concentrated into fewer hands, and controlled by representatives and directors, and yet you sing the old siren song that the workingman should depend entirely upon his own "individual effort."

The school of laissez-faire, of which you seem to be a pronounced advocate, has produced great men in advocating the theory of each for himself and his Satanic majesty taking the hindermost, but the most pronounced advocates of your school of thought in economics have, when practically put to the test, been compelled to admit that combination and organization of the toiling masses are essential both to prevent the deterioration and to secure an improvement in the condition of the wage earners.

If, as you say, the success of commercial society depends upon the full play of competition, why do not you and your confreres turn your attention and direct the shafts of your attacks against the trusts and corporations, business wreckers and manipulators in the food products—the necessities of the people. Why garland your thoughts in beautiful phrase when speaking of these modern vampires, and steep your pen in gall when writing of the laborers' efforts to secure some of the advantages accruing from the concentrated thought and genius of the ages?

You charge that before a boy can learn a trade he must receive a permit from the union and assume obligations which the union imposes. I am sure you have read the current history of industry but superficially, or you would certainly have discovered that with the introduction of modern methods of production, the apprenticeship system has almost been entirely eliminated. Professors, the learned men concerned in the welfare of our people, insist upon a maintenance of a technical knowledge of crafts and trades. They are endeavoring to substitute manual training schools in order that the youth of our country may be supplied with a knowledge of the trades and crafts of which modern methods of production have deprived them.

For the sake of your argument, let me admit that what you may say in connection with this matter is true. I ask you whether it is not true that before a boy can properly learn your trade, is it not necessary for him to enter a term of apprenticeship? Of course, you have a more euphonious name for it, student life, I believe. Would judges permit anyone to practise law in their courts where justice is dispensed (with) unless he could produce his working card? Pardon, I mean his diploma.

One becomes enraptured in reading the beauty of your description of modern progress. Could you have had in mind the miners of Spring Valley or Pennsylvania, or the clothing workers of the sweatshops of New York or Chicago when you grandiloquently dilate,

Who is not rich today when compared with his ancestors of a century ago? The steamboat and the railroad bring to his breakfast table the coffees of Java and Brazil, the fruits from Florida and California, and the steaks from the plains. The loom arrays him in garments and the factories furnish him with a dwelling that the richest contemporaries of his grandfather would have envied. With health and industry he is a prince.

Probably you have not read within the past year of babes dying of starvation at their mothers' breasts. More than likely the thousands of men lying upon the bare stones night after night in the City Hall of Chicago last winter escaped your notice. You may not have heard of the cry for bread that was sounded through this land of plenty by thousands of honest men and women. But should these and many other painful incidents have passed you by unnoticed, I am fearful that you may learn of them with keener thoughts with the coming sleets and blasts of winter.

You say that "labor cannot afford to attack capital." Let me remind you that labor has no quarrel with capital, as such. It is merely the possessors of capital who refuse to accord to labor the recognition, the right, the justice which is the laborers' due with whom we contend.

See what is implied by your contemptuous reference to the laborer when you ask, "Will the conqueror destroy his trophy?" Who ever heard of a conqueror marching unitedly with his trophy, as you would have them? But if by your comparison you mean that the conqueror is the corporation, the trust, the capitalist class, and ask then whether they would destroy their trophy, I would have you ask the widows and orphans of the thousands of men killed annually through the avarice of railroad corporations refusing to avail themselves of modern appliances in coupling and other improvements on their railroads.

Inquire from the thousands of women and children whose husbands or fathers were suffocated or crushed in the mines through the rapacious greed of stockholders clamoring for more dividends. Investigate the sweating dens of the large cities. Go to the mills, factories, through the country. Visit the modern tenement houses or hovels in which thousands of workers are compelled to eke out an existence. Ask these whether the conqueror (monopoly) cares whether his trophy (the laborers) is destroyed or preserved. Ascertain from employers whether the laborer is not regarded the same as a machine, thrown out as soon as all the work possible has been squeezed out of him.

Are you aware that all the legislation ever secured for the ventilation or safety of mines, factory, or workshop is the result of the efforts of organized labor? Do you know that the trade unions were the shield for the seven-year-old children from being the conqueror's trophy until they become somewhat older? And that the reformatory laws now on the statute books protecting or defending the trophies of both sexes, young and old from the fond care of the conquerors were wrested from congresses, legislatures, and parliaments despite the Pullmans, the Jeffries, the Ricks, the Tafts, the Williams, the Woods, or the Grosscups.

By what right, sir, do you assume that the labor organizations do not conduct their affairs within lawful limits, or that they are a menace to the lawful institutions of the country? Is it because some thoughtless or overzealous member at a time of great excitement and smarting under a wrong may violate under a law or commit an improper act? Would you apply the same rule to the churches, the other moral agencies and organizations that you do to the organizations of labor? If you did, the greatest moral force of life today, the trade unions, would certainly stand out the clearest, brightest, and purest. Because a certain class (for which you and a number of your colleagues on the bench seem to be the special pleaders) have a monopoly in their lines of trade, I submit that this is no good reason for their claim to have a monopoly on true patriotism or respect for the lawful institutions of the country.

But speaking of law reminds me of the higher law of the land. The Constitution prescribes that all rights not specifically granted to the general government are reserved to the states. There is another provision prohibiting the President from sending armed forces into any state except for the purpose of maintaining "a republican form of government," and then only upon the requisition of the legislature of the state, or of the governor when the legislature is not in session. Yet when, during the recent railroad strike, the President sent the troops into Illinois, it was not in compliance with the request of the legislature of that state, nor of the governor, but in spite of his protest. Yes, even when the governor remonstrated he was practically told by the President to stop arguing the law upon the question. Pardon the simplicity of my inquiry, but does not the law require that its limits shall be observed by a president, a judge, equally as by a labor organization?

If I remember aright you based the injunctions recently issued by you upon the provisions of the Interstate Commerce Law, a law enacted by Congress upon the demand of the farmers and shippers of our country to protect them against the unjust and outrageous discriminations imposed by the railroads. Where in the law can you find one word to justify your course applying to workingmen organized and engaged in a strike?

Read the discussions in Congress when that law was under consideration. You will not find a remote reference to the application of the laws as you construe it. In fact, I am informed upon excellent authority that when the law was before the Senate in the form of a bill, Senator Morgan, of Alabama, proposed an amendment which, if adopted, would have had the effect of empowering judges to issue an order of the nature you have in the recent railroad strike; but it was not adopted; it was defeated. How then in the face of this you can issue your omnibus restraining order passes the comprehension of ordinary men.

In his last report to Congress, the postmaster general recommended the passage of a law by Congress declaring that any train in which there should be but one pouch of mail matter should be considered a mail train, thus recognizing that there was no law by which other than regular "mail trains" come under the operation of the postal laws. Hence it is not a grave stretch of the imagination to regard this latest court-made law as an invention to break the strike.

I am not versed in the law, but somewhere I read that Blackstone says that a law which is not based on justice is not law, and presumably judges who distort law so that injustice is done are not the ablest or purest devotees of the "blind goddess." I do not quote this for the purpose of converting your mind to some degree of impartiality for labor, but merely to show what a sycophantic knave Blackstone was.

Year by year man's liberties are trampled underfoot at the bidding of corporations and trusts, rights are invaded, and law perverted. In all ages, wherever a tyrant has shown himself, he has always found some willing judge to clothe that tyranny in the robes of legality, and modern capitalism has proven no exception to the rule.

You may not know that the labor movement as represented by the trades unions stands for right, for justice, for liberty. You may not imagine that the issuance of an injunction depriving men of a legal as well as a natural right to protect themselves, their wives, and little ones must fail of its purpose. Repression or oppression never yet succeeded in crushing the truth or redressing a wrong.

In conclusion let me assure you that labor will organize and more compactly than ever and upon practical lines; and despite relentless antagonism, achieve for humanity a nobler manhood, a more beautiful womanhood, and a happier childhood.

WOODROW WILSON: THE DECLINING PRESTIGE OF THE PRESIDENTIAL OFFICE (1885)

Source: *Congressional Government: A Study in American Politics*, Boston, 1885, pp. 1–57.

We are the first Americans to hear our own countrymen ask whether the Constitution is still adapted to serve the purposes for which it was intended;

the first to entertain any serious doubts about the superiority of our own institutions as compared with the systems of Europe; the first to think of remodeling the administrative machinery of the federal government and of forcing new forms of responsibility upon Congress.

The evident explanation of this change of attitude toward the Constitution is that we have been made conscious, by the rude shock of the war and by subsequent developments of policy, that there has been a vast alteration in the conditions of government; that the checks and balances which once obtained are no longer. effective; and that we are really living under a Constitution essentially different from that which we have been so long worshiping as our own peculiar and incomparable possession. In short, this model government is no longer conformable with its own original pattern. While we have been shielding it from criticism it has slipped away from us.

The noble charter of fundamental law given us by the convention of 1787 is still our Constitution; but it is now our form of government rather in name than in reality, the form of the Constitution being one of nicely adjusted, ideal balances, while the actual form of our present government is simply a scheme of congressional supremacy. National legislation, of course, takes force now as at first from the authority of the Constitution; but it would be easy to reckon by the score acts of Congress which can by no means be squared with that great instrument's evident theory. We continue to think, indeed, according

to long-accepted constitutional formulas, and it is still politically unorthodox to depart from old-time phraseology in grave discussions of affairs; but it is plain to those who look about them that most of the commonly received opinions concerning federal constitutional balances and administrative arrangements are many years behind the actual practices of the government at Washington, and that we are farther than most of us realize from the times and the policy of the framers of the Constitution.

It is a commonplace observation of historians that, in the development of constitutions, names are much more persistent than the functions upon which they were originally bestowed; that institutions constantly undergo essential alterations of character while retaining the names conferred upon them in their first estate; and the history of our own Constitution is but another illustration of this universal principle of institutional change. There has been a constant growth of legislative and administrative practice, and a steady accretion of precedent in the management of federal affairs, which have broadened the sphere and altered the functions of the government without perceptibly affecting the vocabulary of our constitutional language....

It is said that there is no single or central force in our federal scheme; and so there is not in the federal scheme, but only a balance of powers and a nice adjustment of interactive checks, as all the books say. How is it, however, in the practical conduct of the federal government? In that, unquestionably, the predominant and controlling force, the center and source of all motive and of all regulative power, is Congress. All niceties of constitutional restriction and even many broad principles of constitutional limitation have been overridden and a thoroughly organized system of congressional control set up, which gives a very rude negative to some theories of balance and some schemes for distributed powers, but which suits well with convenience and does violence to none of the principles of self-government contained in the Constitution....

Besides, in ordinary times it is not from the executive that the most dangerous encroachments are to be apprehended. The legislature is the aggressive spirit. It is the motive power of the government, and unless the judiciary can check it, the courts are of comparatively little worth as balance wheels in the system. It is the subtle, stealthy, almost imperceptible encroachments of policy, of political action, which constitute the precedents upon which additional prerogatives are generally reared; and yet these are the very encroachments with which it is hardest for the courts to deal and concerning which, accordingly, the federal courts have declared themselves unauthorized to hold any opinions. They have naught to say upon questions of policy. Congress must itself judge what measures may legitimately be used to supplement or make effectual its acknowledged jurisdiction, what are the laws "necessary and proper for carrying

into execution" its own peculiar powers, "and all other powers vested by" the "Constitution in the government of the United States, or in any department or officer thereof."

The courts are very quick and keen-eyed, too, to discern prerogatives of political discretion in legislative acts, and exceedingly slow to undertake to discriminate between what is and what is not a violation of the spirit of the Constitution. Congress must wantonly go very far outside of the plain and unquestionable meaning of the Constitution, must bump its head directly against all right and precedent, must kick against the very pricks of all well-established rulings and interpretations, before the Supreme Court will offer it any distinct rebuke. ...

But, besides and above all this, the national courts are for the most part in the power of Congress. Even the Supreme Court is not beyond its control; for it is the legislative privilege to increase, whenever the legislative will so pleases, the number of the judges upon the supreme bench—to "dilute the Constitution," as Webster once put it, "by creating a court which shall construe away its provisions"; and this on one memorable occasion it did choose to do....

It is noteworthy that Mr. Adams, possibly because he had himself been President, describes the executive as constituting only "in some degree" a check upon Congress, though he puts no such limitation upon the other balances of the system. Independently of experience, however, it might reasonably have been expected that the prerogatives of the President would have been one of the most effectual restraints upon the power of Congress. He was constituted one of the three great coordinate branches of the government; his functions were made of the highest dignity; his privileges many and substantial — so great, indeed, that it has pleased the fancy of some writers to parade them as exceeding those of the British Crown. And there can be little doubt that had the presidential chair always been filled by men of commanding character, of acknowledged ability, and of thorough political training, it would have continued to be a seat of the highest authority and consideration, the true center of the federal structure, the real throne of administration, and the frequent source of policies. Washington and his cabinet commanded the ear of Congress and gave shape to its deliberations; Adams, though often crossed and thwarted, gave character to the government; and Jefferson, as President no less than as secretary of state, was the real leader of his party. But the prestige of the presidential office has declined with the character of the Presidents. And the character of the Presidents has declined as the perfection of selfish party tactics has advanced....

I am disposed to think, however, that the decline in the character of the Presidents is not the cause but only the accompanying manifestation of the declining prestige of the presidential office. That high office has fallen from its first estate of dignity because

its power has waned; and its power has waned because the power of Congress has become predominant. The early Presidents were...men of such a stamp that they would under any circumstances have made their influence felt; but their opportunities were exceptional. What with quarreling and fighting with England, buying Louisiana and Florida, building dikes to keep out the flood of the French Revolution, and extricating the country from ceaseless broils with the South American republics, the government was...constantly busy, during the first quarter century of its existence, with the adjustment of foreign relations; and with foreign relations, of course, the Presidents had everything to do, since theirs was the office of negotiation.

Moreover, as regards home policy, also, those times were not like ours. Congress was somewhat awkward in exercising its untried powers, and its machinery was new and without that fine adjustment which has since made it perfect of its kind. Not having as yet learned the art of governing itself to the best advantage, and being without that facility of legislation which it afterward acquired, the legislature was glad to get guidance and suggestions of policy from the executive.

But this state of things did not last long. Congress was very quick and apt in learning what it could do and in getting into thoroughly good trim to do it. It very early divided itself into standing committees which it equipped with very comprehensive and thoroughgoing privileges of legislative initiative and control, and set itself through these to administer the government....

The executive was losing and Congress gaining weight; and the station to which cabinets finally attained was a station of diminished and diminishing power. There is no distincter tendency in congressional history than the tendency to subject even the details of administration to the constant supervision, and all policy to the watchful intervention, of the standing committees.

I am inclined to think, therefore, that the enlarged powers of Congress are the fruits rather of an immensely increased efficiency of organization, and of the redoubled activity consequent upon the facility of action secured by such organization, than of any definite and persistent scheme of conscious usurpation. It is safe to say that Congress always had the desire to have a hand in every affair of federal government; but it was only by degrees that it found means and opportunity to gratify that desire; and its activity, extending its bounds wherever perfected processes of congressional work offered favoring prospects, has been enlarged so naturally and so silently that it has almost always seemed of normal extent, and has never, except perhaps during one or two brief periods of extraordinary political disturbance, appeared to reach much beyond its acknowledged constitutional sphere....

What makes it the more important to understand the present mechanism of national government, and to study the methods of congressional rule in a light unclouded by theory, is that there is plain evidence that the expansion of federal power is to continue, and that there exists, consequently, an evident necessity that it should be known just what to do and how to do it when the time comes for public opinion to take control of the forces which are changing the character of our Constitution....

Unquestionably, the pressing problems of the present moment regard the regulation of our vast systems of commerce and manufacture, the control of giant corporations, the restraint of monopolies, the perfection of fiscal arrangements, the facilitating of economic exchanges, and many other like national concerns, among which may possibly be numbered the question of marriage and divorce; and the greatest of these problems do not fall within even the enlarged sphere of the federal government. Some of them can be embraced within its jurisdiction by no possible stretch of construction, and the majority of them only by wresting the Constitution to strange and as yet unimagined uses. Still there is a distinct movement in favor of national control of all questions of policy which manifestly demand uniformity of treatment and power of administration such as cannot be realized by the separate, unconcerted action of the states; and it seems probable to many that, whether by constitutional amendment or by still further flights of construction, yet broader territory will at no very distant day be assigned to the federal government.

It becomes a matter of the utmost importance, therefore, both for those who would arrest this tendency and for those who, because they look upon it with allowance if not with positive favor, would let it run its course, to examine critically the government upon which this new weight of responsibility and power seems likely to be cast, in order that its capacity both for the work it now does and for that which it may be called upon to do may be definitely estimated.

RUTHERFORD B. HAYES: WEALTH IN THE HANDS OF THE FEW (1886–87)

Source: *Diary and Letters of Rutherford Birchard Hayes*, Charles R. Williams, ed., Vol. IV, Columbus, O., 1924, pp. 261–262, 277–278, 286, 312, 354–355.

January 22, 1886. Friday. How to distribute more equally the property of our country is a question we (Theodore Clapp and I) considered yesterday. We ought not to allow a permanent aristocracy of inherited wealth to grow up in our country. How would it answer to limit the amount that could be left to any one person by will or otherwise? What should be the limit? Let no one receive from another more than the law gives to the chief justice, to the general of the Army, or to the president of the Senate. Let the income of the property transmitted equal this, say $10,000 to $20,000. If after distributing on this principle there remains undistributed part of the estate, let it go to the public. The object is to secure a distribution of great estates to prevent accumulation.

January 24. Sunday. The question for the country now is how to secure a more equal distribution of property among the people. There can be no republican institutions with vast masses of property permanently in a few hands, and large masses of voters without property. To begin the work, as a first step, prevent large estates from passing, by wills or by inheritance or by corporations, into the hands of a single man. Let no man get by inheritance or by will more than will produce at 4 percent interest an income equal to the salary paid to the chief justice, to the general of the Army, or to the highest officer of the Navy — say an income of $15,000 per year or an estate of $500,000....

March 17. Wednesday. I go to Toledo to attend the celebration of St. Patrick's Day by Father Hannan's people. I shall talk to the text, "America, the Land of the Free and the Home of the Brave," with special reference to Father Hannan's motto "Religion, Education, Temperance, Industry"; and this again in behalf of such measures and laws as will give to every workingman a reasonable hope that by industry, temperance, and frugality he can secure a home for himself and his family, education for his children, and a comfortable support for old age.

March 18. Thursday. At Toledo yesterday and until 1 p.m. today. At Father Hannan's St. Patrick's Institute last evening. I spoke of the danger from riches in a few hands, and the poverty of the masses. The capital and labor question. General Comly regards the speech as important. My point is that free government cannot long endure if property is largely in a few hands and large masses of the people are unable to earn homes, education, and a support in old age....

March 19. Friday. No man, however benevolent, liberal, and wise, can use a large fortune so that it will do half as much good in the world as it would if it were divided into moderate sums and in the hands of workmen who had earned it by industry and frugality. The piling up of estates often does great and conspicuous good. Such men as Benjamin Franklin and Peter Cooper knew how to use wealth. But no man does with accumulated wealth so much good as the same amount would do in many hands.

March 20. Saturday. The funeral of General Devereux (at Cleveland today) was largely attended. With General Leggett, General Barnett, and General Elwell, and many others of the Loyal Legion—those named as honorary pallbearers—saw and heard all that belonged to the impressive funeral. The leading traits of General Devereux were unusual tact in dealing with all sorts of men and all sorts of difficult questions, courage, and integrity. The president of the New York Central, Mr. (Chauncey M.) Depew, introduced me to Cornelius Vanderbilt. I could not help regarding him with sympathy. One of our Republican kings—one of our railroad kings. Think of the inconsistency of allowing such vast and irresponsible power as

he possesses to be vested by law in the hands of one man!

March 26. Friday. Am I mistaken in thinking that we are drawing near the time when we must decide to limit and control great wealth, corporations, and the like, or resort to a strong military government? Is this the urgent question? I read in the (Cleveland) Leader of this morning that Rev. Dr. Washington Gladden lectured in Cleveland last night on "Capital and Labor." Many good things were said. The general drift and spirit were good. But he leaves out our railroad system. Shall the railroads govern the country, or shall the people govern the railroads? Shall the interest of railroad kings be chiefly regarded, or shall the interest of the people be paramount?

May 12. On the labor question, my position is: 1. The previous question always must be in any popular excitement the supremacy of law. All lawless violence must be suppressed instantly, with overwhelming force and at all hazards. To hesitate or tamper with it is a fatal mistake. Justice, humanity, and safety all require this. 2. I agree that labor does not get its fair share of the wealth it creates. The Sermon on the Mount, the Golden Rule, the Declaration of Independence, all require extensive reforms to the end that labor may be so rewarded that the workingman can, with temperance, industry, and thrift, own a home, educate his children, and lay up a support for old age. 3. The United States must begin to deal with the whole subject. I approve heartily of President Cleveland's message and so said at the great soldiers' meeting at Cleveland.

February 25, 1887. Friday. As to pensions I would say our Union soldiers fought in the divinest war that was ever waged. Our war did more for our country than any other war ever achieved for any other country. It did more for the world, more for mankind, than any other war in all history. It gave to those who remained at home and to those who come after it in our country opportunities, prosperity, wealth, a future, such as no war ever before conferred on any part of the human race.

No soldier who fought in that war on the right side nor his widow nor his orphans ought ever to be forced to choose between starvation and the poorhouse. Lincoln in his last inaugural address—just before the war closed, when the last enlistments were going on—pledged the nation "to care for him who hath borne the battle and for his widow and his orphans." Let that sacred pledge be sacredly kept.

December 4. Sunday. In church it occurred to me that it is time for the public to hear that the giant evil and danger in this country, the danger which transcends all others, is the vast wealth owned or controlled by a few persons. Money is power. In Congress, in state legislatures, in city councils, in the courts, in the political conventions, in the press, in the pulpit, in the circles of the educated and the talented its influence is growing greater and greater. Excessive wealth in the hands of the few means extreme poverty, ignorance, vice, and wretchedness as the lot of the many. It is not yet time to debate about the remedy.

The previous question is as to the danger—the evil. Let the people be fully informed and convinced as to the evil. Let them earnestly seek the remedy and it will be found. Fully to know the evil is the first step toward reaching its eradication. Henry George is strong when he portrays the rottenness of the present system. We are, to say the least, not yet ready for his remedy. We may reach and remove the difficulty by changes in the laws regulating corporations, descents of property, wills, trusts, taxation, and a host of other important interests, not omitting lands and other property.

GROVER CLEVELAND: SURPLUS REVENUES AND THE TARIFF (1887)

Source: *A Compilation of the Messages and Papers of the Presidents 1789-1897.* James D. Richardson, ed., Washington, reprinted 1900, Vol. VIII, pp. 580–591.

You are confronted at the threshold of your legislative duties with a condition of the national finances which imperatively demands immediate and careful consideration.

The amount of money annually exacted, through the operation of present laws, from the industries and necessities of the people largely exceeds the sum necessary to meet the expenses of the government. When we consider that the theory of our institutions guarantees to every citizen the full enjoyment of all the fruits of his industry and enterprise, with only such deduction as may be his share toward the careful and economical maintenance of the government which protects him, it is plain that the exaction of more than this is indefensible extortion and a culpable betrayal of American fairness and justice. This wrong inflicted upon those who bear the burden of national taxation, like other wrongs, multiplies a brood of evil consequences.

The public Treasury, which should only exist as a conduit conveying the people's tribute to its legitimate objects of expenditure, becomes a hoarding place for money needlessly withdrawn from trade and the people's use, thus crippling our national energies, suspending our country's development, preventing investment in productive enterprise, threatening financial disturbance; and inviting schemes of public plunder. This condition of our Treasury is not altogether new, and it has more than once of late been submitted to the people's representatives in the Congress, who alone can apply a remedy. And yet the situation still continues; with aggravated incidents, more than ever presaging financial convulsion and widespread disaster.

It will not do to neglect this situation because its dangers are not now palpably imminent and apparent. They exist nonetheless certainly, and await the unforeseen and unexpected occasion when suddenly they will be precipitated upon us....

While the functions of our National Treasury should be few and simple, and while its best condition would be reached, I believe, by its entire disconnection with private business interests, yet when, by a perversion of its purposes, it idly holds money uselessly subtracted from the channels of trade, there seems to be reason for the claim that some legitimate means should be devised by the government to restore in an emergency, without waste or extravagance, such money to its place among the people.

If such an emergency arises, there now exists no clear and undoubted executive power of relief. Heretofore the redemption of 3 percent bonds, which were payable at the option of the government, has afforded a means for the disbursement of the excess of our revenues; but these bonds have all been retired, and there are no bonds outstanding, the payment of which we have a right to insist upon. The contribution to the sinking fund which furnishes the occasion for expenditure in the purchase of bonds has been already made for the current year, so that there is no outlet in that direction.

In the present state of legislation, the only pretense of any existing executive power to restore at this time any part of our surplus revenues to the people by its expenditure consists in the supposition that the secretary of the Treasury may enter the market and purchase the bonds of the government not yet due, at a rate of premium to be agreed upon. The only provision of law from which such a power could be derived is found in an appropriation bill passed a number of years ago, and it is subject to the suspicion that it was intended as temporary and limited in its application, instead of conferring a continuing discretion and authority.

No condition ought to exist which would justify the grant of power to a single official, upon his judgment of its necessity, to withhold from or release to the business of the people, in an unusual manner, money held in the Treasury, and thus affect at his will the financial situation of the country; and if it is deemed wise to lodge in the secretary of the Treasury the authority in the present juncture to purchase bonds, it should be plainly vested and provided, as far as possible, with such checks and limitations as will define this official's right and discretion and at the same time relieve him from undue responsibility.

In considering the question of purchasing bonds as a means of restoring to circulation the surplus money accumulating in the Treasury, it should be borne in mind that premiums must of course be paid upon such purchase, that there may be a large part of these bonds held as investments which cannot be purchased at any price, and that combinations among holders who are willing to sell may unreasonably enhance the cost of such bonds to the government.

It has been suggested that the present bonded debt might be refunded at a less rate of interest and the difference between the old and new security paid in cash, thus finding use for the surplus in the Treasury. The success of this plan, it is apparent, must depend upon the volition of the holders of the present bonds; and it is not entirely certain that the inducement which must be offered them would result in more financial benefit to the government than the purchase of bonds, while the latter proposition would reduce the principal of the debt by actual payment instead of extending it.

The proposition to deposit the money held by the government in banks throughout the country for use by the people is, it seems to me, exceedingly objectionable in principle, as establishing too close a relationship between the operations of the government Treasury and the business of the country and too extensive a commingling of their money, thus fostering an unnatural reliance in private business upon public funds. If this scheme should be adopted, it should only be done as a temporary expedient to meet an urgent necessity. Legislative and executive effort should generally be in the opposite direction and should have a tendency to divorce, as much and as fast as can be safely done, the Treasury Department from private enterprise.

Of course it is not expected that unnecessary and extravagant appropriations will be made for the purpose of avoiding the accumulation of an excess of revenue. Such expenditure, besides the demoralization of all just conceptions of public duty which it entails, stimulates a habit of reckless improvidence not in the least consistent with the mission of our people or the high and beneficent purposes of our government.

I have deemed it my duty to thus bring to the knowledge of my countrymen, as well as to the attention of their representatives charged with the responsibility of legislative relief, the gravity of our financial situation. The failure of the Congress heretofore to provide against the dangers which it was quite evident the very nature of the difficulty must necessarily produce caused a condition of financial distress and apprehension since your last adjournment, which taxed to the utmost all the authority and expedients within executive control; and these appear now to be exhausted. If disaster results from the continued inaction of Congress, the responsibility must rest where it belongs....

Our scheme of taxation, by means of which this needless surplus is taken from the people and put into the public Treasury, consists of a tariff or duty levied upon importations from abroad and internal revenue taxes levied upon the consumption of tobacco and spirituous and malt liquors. It must be conceded that none of the things subjected to internal revenue taxation are, strictly speaking, necessaries. There appears to be no just complaint of this taxation by the consumers of these articles, and there seems to be nothing so well able to bear the burden without hardship to any portion of the people.

But our present tariff laws, the vicious, inequitable, and illogical source of unnecessary taxation, ought to be at once revised and amended. These laws, as their primary and plain effect, raise the price to consumers of all articles imported and subject to duty by precisely the sum paid for such duties. Thus the amount of the duty measures the tax paid by those who purchase for use these imported articles. Many of these things, however, are raised or manufactured in our own country, and the duties now levied upon foreign goods and products are called protection to these home manufactures, because they render it possible for those of our people who are manufacturers to make these taxed articles and sell them for a price equal to that demanded for the imported goods that have paid customs duty.

So it happens that while comparatively a few use the imported articles, millions of our people, who never used and never saw any of the foreign products, purchase and use things of the same kind made in this country, and pay therefor nearly or quite the same enhanced price which the duty adds to the imported articles. Those who buy imports pay the duty charged thereon into the public Treasury, but the great majority of our citizens, who buy domestic articles of the same class, pay a sum at least approximately equal to this duty to the home manufacturer. This reference to the operation of our tariff laws is not made by way of instruction but in order that we may be constantly reminded of the manner in which they impose a burden upon those who consume domestic products as well as those who consume imported articles, and thus create a tax upon all our people.

It is not proposed to entirely relieve the country of this taxation. It must be extensively continued as the source of the government's income; and in a readjustment of our tariff the interests of American labor engaged in manufacture should be carefully considered, as well as the preservation of our manufacturers. It may be called protection or by any other name, but relief from the hardships and dangers of our present tariff laws should be devised with especial precaution against imperilling the existence of our manufacturing interests. But this existence should not mean a condition which, without regard to the public welfare or a national exigency, must always insure the realization of immense profits instead of moderately profitable returns. As the volume and diversity of our national activities increase, new recruits are added to those who desire a continuation of the advantages which they conceive the present system of tariff taxation directly affords them. So stubbornly have all efforts to reform the present condition been resisted by those of our fellow citizens thus engaged that they can hardly complain of the suspicion, entertained to a certain extent, that there exists an organized combination all along the line to maintain their advantage.

We are in the midst of centennial celebrations, and with becoming pride we rejoice in American skill and ingenuity, in American energy and enterprise, and in the wonderful natural advantages and resources developed by a century's national growth. Yet when an attempt is made to justify a scheme which permits a tax to be laid upon every consumer in the land for the benefit of our manufacturers, quite beyond a reasonable demand for governmental regard, it suits the purposes of advocacy to call our manufactures infant industries still needing the highest and greatest degree of favor and fostering care that can be wrung from federal legislation.

It is also said that the increase in the price of domestic manufactures resulting from the present tariff is necessary in order that higher wages may be paid to our workingmen employed in manufactories than are paid for what is called the pauper labor of Europe. All will acknowledge the force of an argument which involves the welfare and liberal compensation of our laboring people. Our labor is honorable in the eyes of every American citizen; and as it lies at the foundation of our development and progress, it is entitled, without affectation or hypocrisy, to the utmost regard. The standard of our laborers' life should not be measured by that of any other country less favored, and they are entitled to their full share of all our advantages.

By the last census it is made to appear that of the 17,392,099 of our population engaged in all kinds of industries, 7,670,493 are employed in agriculture, 4,074,238 in professional and personal service (2,934,876 of whom are domestic servants and laborers), while 1,810,256 are employed in trade and transportation, and 3,837,112 are classed as employed in manufacturing and mining....

The farmer and the agriculturist, who manufacture nothing, but who pay the increased price which the tariff imposes upon every agricultural implement, upon all he wears, and upon all he uses and owns, except the increase of his flocks and herds and such things as his husbandry produces from the soil, is invited to aid in maintaining the present situation; and he is told that a high duty on imported wool is necessary for the benefit of those who have sheep to shear in order that the price of their wool may be increased. They, of course, are not reminded that the farmer who has no sheep is by this scheme obliged, in his purchases of clothing and woolen goods, to pay a tribute to his fellow farmer as well as to the manufacturer and merchant, nor is any mention made of the fact that the sheep owners themselves and their households must wear clothing and use other articles manufactured from the wool they sell at tariff prices, and thus as consumers must return their share of this increased price to the tradesman....

In speaking of the increased cost to the consumer of our home manufactures resulting from a duty laid upon imported articles of the same description, the fact is not overlooked that competition among our domestic producers sometimes has the effect of keeping the price of their products below the highest limit allowed by such duty. But it is notorious that this competition is too often strangled by combinations quite prevalent at this time, and frequently called trusts, which have for their object the regulation of the supply and price of commodities made and sold by members of the combination. The people can hardly hope for any consideration in the operation of these selfish schemes.

If, however, in the absence of such combination, a healthy and free competition reduces the price of any particular dutiable article of home production below the limit which it might otherwise reach under our tariff laws, and if with such reduced price its manufacture continues to thrive, it is entirely evident that one thing has been discovered which should be carefully scrutinized in an effort to reduce taxation.

The necessity of combination to maintain the price of any commodity to the tariff point furnishes proof that someone is willing to accept lower prices for such commodity and that such prices are remunerative; and lower prices produced by competition prove the same thing. Thus where either of these conditions exists a case would seem to be presented for an easy reduction of taxation.

The considerations which have been presented touching our tariff laws are intended only to enforce an earnest recommendation that the surplus revenues of the government be prevented by the reduction of our customs duties, and at the same time to emphasize a suggestion that in accomplishing this purpose we may discharge a double duty to our people by granting to them a measure of relief from tariff taxation in quarters where it is most needed and from sources where it can be most fairly and justly accorded.

Nor can the presentation made of such considerations be with any degree of fairness regarded as evidence of unfriendliness toward our manufacturing interests or of any lack of appreciation of their value and importance. These interests constitute a leading and most substantial element of our national greatness and furnish the proud proof of our country's progress. But, if in the emergency that presses upon us, our manufacturers are asked to surrender something for the public good and to avert disaster, their patriotism, as well as a grateful recognition of advantages already afforded, should lead them to willing cooperation.

No demand is made that they shall forego all the benefits of governmental regard; but they cannot fail to be admonished of their duty, as well as their enlightened self-interest and safety, when they are reminded of the fact that financial panic and collapse, to which the present condition tends, afford no greater shelter or protection to our manufactures than to other important enterprises. Opportunity for safe, careful, and deliberate reform is now offered; and none of us should be unmindful of a time when an abused and irritated people, heedless of those who have resisted timely and reasonable relief, may insist upon a radical and sweeping rectification of their wrongs.

The difficulty attending a wise and fair revision of our tariff laws is not underestimated. It will require on the part of the Congress great labor and care, and especially a broad and national contemplation of the subject and a patriotic disregard of such local and selfish claims as are unreasonable and reckless of the welfare of the entire country.

Under our present laws more than 4,000 articles are subject to duty. Many of these do not in any way compete with our own manufactures, and many are hardly worth attention as subjects of revenue. A considerable reduction can be made in the aggregate by adding them to the free list. The taxation of luxuries presents no features of hardship; but the necessaries of life used and consumed by all the people, the duty upon which adds to the cost of living in every home, should be greatly cheapened.

The radical reduction of the duties imposed upon raw material used in manufactures, or its free importation, is of course an important factor in any effort to reduce the price of these necessaries. It would not only relieve them from the increased cost caused by the tariff on such material but the manufactured product, being thus cheapened, that part of the tariff now laid upon such product, as a compensation to our manufacturers for the present price of raw material could be accordingly modified. Such reduction or free importation would serve besides to largely reduce the revenue.

It is not apparent how such a change can have any injurious effect upon our manufacturers. On the contrary, it would appear to give them a better chance in foreign markets with the manufacturers of other countries, who cheapen their wares by free material. Thus our people might have the opportunity of extending their sales beyond the limits of home consumption, saving them from the depression, interruption in business, and loss caused by a glutted domestic market and affording their employees more certain and steady labor, with its resulting quiet and contentment.

The question thus imperatively presented for solution should be approached in a spirit higher than partisanship and considered in the light of that regard for patriotic duty which should characterize the action of those entrusted with the weal of a confiding people. But the obligation to declared party policy and principle is not wanting to urge prompt and effective action. Both of the great political parties now represented in the government have by repeated and authoritative declarations condemned the condition of our laws which permit the collection from the people of unnecessary revenue, and have in the most solemn manner promised its correction; and neither as citizens nor partisans are our countrymen in a mood to condone the deliberate violation of these pledges.

Our progress toward a wise conclusion will not be improved by dwelling upon the theories of protection and free trade. This savors too much of bandying epithets. It is a condition which confronts us, not a theory. Relief from this condition may involve a slight reduction of the advantages which we award our home productions, but the entire withdrawal of such advantages should not be contemplated. The question of free trade is absolutely irrelevant, and the persistent claim made in certain quarters that all the efforts to relieve the people from unjust and unnecessary taxation are schemes of so-called free traders is mischievous and far removed from any consideration for the public good.

The simple and plain duty which we owe the people is to reduce taxation to the necessary expenses of an economical operation of the government and to restore to the business of the country the money which we hold in the Treasury through the perversion of governmental powers. These things can and should be done with safety to all our industries, without danger to the opportunity for remunerative labor which our workingmen need, and with benefit to them and all our people by cheapening their means of subsistence and increasing the measure of their comforts.

THE SHERMAN ANTITRUST ACT (1890)

Source: *The Public Statutes at Large of the United States of America*, Washington, 1891, Vol. XXVI, pp. 209–210.

An act to protect trade and commerce against unlawful restraints and monopolies.

Be it enacted by the Senate and House of Representatives of the United States of America in Congress assembled:

Section 1. Every contract, combination in the form of trust or otherwise, or conspiracy in restraint of trade or commerce among the several states or with foreign nations is hereby declared to be illegal. Every person who shall make any such contract or engage in any such combination or conspiracy shall be deemed guilty of a misdemeanor, and on conviction thereof shall be punished by fine not exceeding $5,000 or by imprisonment not exceeding one year, or by both said punishments, in the discretion of the court.

Section 2. Every person who shall monopolize, or attempt to monopolize, or combine or conspire with any other person or persons to monopolize any part of the trade or commerce among the several states or with foreign nations shall be deemed guilty of a misdemeanor, and on conviction thereof shall be punished by fine not exceeding $5,000 or by imprisonment not exceeding one year, or by both said punishments, in the discretion of the court.

Section 3. Every contract, combination in form of trust or otherwise, or conspiracy in restraint of trade or commerce in any territory of the United States or of the District of Columbia, or in restraint of trade or commerce between any such territory and another, or between any such territory or territories and any state or states or the District of Columbia, or with foreign nations, or between the District of Columbia and any state or states or foreign nations is hereby declared illegal. Every person who shall make any such contract or engage in any such combination or conspiracy shall be deemed guilty of a misdemeanor,

and on conviction thereof shall be punished by fine not exceeding $5,000 or by imprisonment not exceeding one year, or by both said punishments, in the discretion of the court.

Section 4. The several Circuit courts of the United States are hereby invested with jurisdiction to prevent and restrain violations of this act; and it shall be the duty of the several district attorneys of the United States, in their respective districts, under the direction of the attorney general, to institute proceedings in equity to prevent and restrain such violations. Such proceedings may be by way of petition setting forth the case and praying that such violations shall be enjoined or otherwise prohibited. When the parties complained of shall have been duly notified of such petition, the court shall proceed, as soon as may be, to the hearing and determination of the case; and, pending such petition and before final decree, the court may at any time make such temporary restraining order or prohibition as shall be deemed just in the premises.

Section 5. Whenever it shall appear to the court before which any proceeding under Section 4 of this act may be pending, that the ends of justice require that other parties should be brought before the court, the court may cause them to be summoned, whether they reside in the district in which the court is held or not; and subpoenas to that end may be served in any district by the marshal thereof.

Section 6. Any property owned under any contract or by any combination, or pursuant to any conspiracy (and being the subject thereof) mentioned in Section 1 of this act, and being in the course of transportation from one state to another or to a foreign country, shall be forfeited to the United States, and may be seized and condemned by like proceedings as those provided by law for the forfeiture, seizure, and condemnation of property imported into the United States contrary to law.

Section 7. Any person who shall be injured in his business or property by any other person or corporation by reason of anything forbidden or declared to be unlawful by this act may sue therefor in any Circuit Court of the United States in the district in which the defendant resides or is found, without respect to the amount in controversy, and shall recover threefold the damages by him sustained, and the costs of suit, including a reasonable attorney's fee.

Section 8. That the word "person," or "persons," wherever used in this act, shall be deemed to include corporations and associations existing under or authorized by the laws of either the United States, the laws of any of the territories, the laws of any state, or the laws of any foreign country.

HAMILTON S. WICKS: THE OKLAHOMA LAND RUSH (1889)

Source: *Cosmopolitan*, September 1889: "The Opening of Oklahoma."

A city established and populated in half a day, in a remote region of country and many miles distant from the nearest civilized community, is a marvel that could have been possible in no age but our own, and in no land except the United States.

The opening of Oklahoma was indeed one of the most important events that has occurred in the development of the West. It marks an epoch in the settlement of the unoccupied lands owned by the government of the United States. Never before has there been such a general uprising of the common people seeking homesteads upon the few remaining acres possessed by Uncle Sam. The conditions and circumstances of the settlement of Oklahoma were widely different from those of the settlement of any other section of the United States. This new territory is surrounded by thoroughly settled and well-organized commonwealths. It is a region containing an area of 69,000 square miles, having an average width of 470 miles, and an average length of 210 miles, being much larger than Ohio, or Indiana, or Kentucky, or Illinois, or "the Virginias," or even the whole of New England.

No method can so clearly bring before the public the actual facts of this wonderful opening as the narration, by one who participated in it, of his experience....

As our train slowly moved through the Cherokee Strip, a vast procession of "boomers" was seen moving across the plains to the Oklahoma lines, forming picturesque groups on the otherwise unbroken landscape. The wagon road through the "Strip," extemporized by the boomers, ran for long distances parallel with the railway, and the procession that extended the whole distance illustrated the characteristics of Western American life. Here, for instance, would be a party consisting of a "prairie schooner" drawn by four scrawny, raw-boned horses, and filled with a tatterdemalion group, consisting of a shaggy bearded man, a slatternly looking woman, and several girls and boys, faithful images of their parents, in shabby attire, usually with a dog and a coop of chickens. In striking contrast to this frontier picture, perhaps a couple of flashy real estate men from Wichita would come jogging on a short distance behind, driving a spanking span of bays, with an equipage looking for all the world as though it had just come from a fashionable livery stable.

Our train, whirling rapidly over the prairie, overtook many such contrasted pictures. There were single rigs and double rigs innumerable; there were six-mule teams and four-in-hands, with here and there parties on horseback, and not a few on foot trudging along the way-side. The whole procession marched, rode, or drove, as on some gala occasion, with smiling faces and waving hands. Everyone imagined that Eldorado was just ahead, and I dare say the possibility of failure or disappointment did not enter into the consideration of a single individual on that cool and delightful April day.

For many, alas, the anticipations were "April hopes, the fools of chance."

As our train neared the Oklahoma border, the "procession" became more dense and in some instances clogged the approaches to the fords of the small streams that crossed its pathway. When we finally slowed up at the dividing line, the camps of the "boomers" could be seen extending in every direction, and a vast amount of stock was strewn over the green prairie.

And now the hour of twelve was at hand, and everyone on the qui vive for the bugle blast that would dissolve the chain of enchantment hitherto gird-ing about this coveted land. Many of the "boomers" were mounted on high-spirited and fleet-footed horses, and had ranged themselves along the territorial line, scarcely restrained even by the pres-ence of the troop of cavalry from taking summary possession. The better class of wagons and carriages ranged themselves in line with the horsemen, and even here and there mule teams attached to canvas-covered vehicles stood in the front ranks, with the reins and whip grasped by the "boomers" wives. All was excitement and expectation. Every nerve was on tension and every muscle strained. The great event for which these brawny noblemen of the West have been waiting for years was on the point of transpiring.

Suddenly the air was pierced with the blast of a bugle. Hundreds of throats echoed the sound with shouts of exul-tation. The quivering limbs of saddled steeds, no longer restrained by the hands that held their bridles, bounded forward simultaneously into the "beautiful land" of Oklahoma; and wagons and carriages and buggies and prairie schooners and a whole congregation of curious equipages joined in this unparalleled race, where every starter was bound to win a prize—the "Realization Stakes" of home and prosperity.

Here was a unique contest in which thousands participated and which was to occur but once for all time. Truly an historical event! We, the spectators, witnessed the spectacle with most intense interest. Away dashed the thoroughbreds, the broncos, the pintos, and the mustangs at a breakneck pace across the uneven surface of the prairie. It was amazing to witness the recklessness of those cowboy riders. They jumped obstacles; they leaped ditches; they cantered with no diminution of speed through water pools; and when they came to a ravine too wide to leap, down they would go with a rush, and up the other side with a spurt of energy, to scurry once more like mad over the level plain. This reckless riding was all very well at the fore part of the race, but it could not prevail against the more discreet maneuverings of several elderly "boomers" who rode more powerful and speedy horses.

One old white-bearded fellow especially commanded attention. He was mounted on a coal black thoroughbred, and avoided any disaster by checking the pace of his animal when ravines had to be crossed. But his splendid bursts of speed when no obstructions barred the way soon placed him far in advance of all his competitors. It took but a short time to solve this question of speed among the riders, and after a neck-and-neck race for half a mile or more, they spread like a fan over the prairie, and were eventually lost to our vision among the rolling billows of Oklahoma's far-expanding prairie....

The race was not over when you reached the particular lot you were content to select for your possession. The contest still was who should drive their stakes first, who would erect their little tents soonest, and then, who would quickest build a little wooden shanty.

The situation was so peculiar that it is difficult to convey correct impressions of the situation. It reminded me of playing blindman's buff. One did not know how far to go before stopping; it was hard to tell when it was best to stop; and it was a puzzle whether to turn to the right hand or the left. Everyone appeared dazed, and all for the most part acted like a flock of stray sheep. Where the boldest led, many others followed. I found myself, without exactly knowing how, about midway between the government building and depot. It occurred to me that a street would probably run past the depot.

I accosted a man who looked like a deputy, with a piece of white cord in his hands, and asked him if this was to be a street along here.

"Yes," he replied. "We are laying off four corner lots right here for a lumber yard."

"Is this the corner where I stand?" I inquired.

"Yes," he responded, approaching me.

"Then I claim this corner lot!" I said with decision, as I jammed my location stick in the ground and hammered it securely home with my heel. "I propose to have one lot at all hazards on this town site, and you will have to limit yourself to three, in this location at least."

An angry altercation ensued, but I stoutly maintained my position and my rights. I proceeded at once to unstrap a small folding cot I brought with me, and, by standing it on its end, it made a tolerable center pole for a tent. I then threw a couple of my blankets over the cot and staked them securely into the ground on either side. Thus I had a claim that was unjumpable because of substantial improvements, and I felt safe and breathed more freely until my brother arrived on the third train, with our tent and equipments.

Not long after his arrival, an enterprising individual came driving by with a plow, and we hired him for a dollar to plow around the lot I had stepped off, 25 feet in front and 140 feet in depth. Before dusk we had a large wall tent erected on our newly acquired premises, with a couple of cots inside and a liberal amount of blankets for bedding. Now we felt doubly secure in our possession; and as night approached, I strolled up on the eminence near the Land Office and surveyed the wonderful cyclorama spread out before me on all sides.

Ten thousand people had "squatted" upon a square mile of virgin prairie that first afternoon, and as the myriad of white tents suddenly appeared upon the face of the country, it was as though a vast flock of huge white-winged birds had just settled down upon the hillsides and in the valleys. Here indeed was a city laid out and populated in half a day. Thousands of campfires sparkled upon the dark bosom of the prairie as far as the eye could reach, and there arose from this huge camp a subdued hum declaring that this almost innumerable multitude of the brave and self-reliant men had come to stay and work and build in that distant Western wilderness a city that should forever be a trophy to American enterprise and daring....

On the morning of April 23, a city of 10,000 people, 500 houses, and innumerable tents existed where twelve hours before was nothing but a broad expanse of prairie. The new city changed its appearance every twenty-four hours, as day by day the work of construction went on. The tents were rapidly superseded by small frame structures, until at the end of a month there were scarcely any tents to be seen. The small frame structures in turn gave place to larger ones, and a number of fine two-story frame buildings were erected on the principal thoroughfares before the end of the first sixty days. The cost of these two-story frame buildings ranged from $700 to $2,000, where lumber was purchased at $30 per thousand and carpenters charged $3 a day.

As soon as it became apparent to capitalists that this enterprise was in reality the beginnings of a great city, preparations were made for the erection of a number of brick blocks; and at the time of writing this article—less than one hundred days from the date of the opening—Guthrie presents the appearance of a model Western city, with broad and regular streets and alleys; with handsome store and office buildings; with a system of parks and boulevards, unsurpassed in point of number, extent, and beauty by any city of twice its size and population in the West; with a number of fine iron bridges spanning the Cottonwood River, which runs through its midst; with a system of waterworks that furnishes hydrants at the corners of all the principal streets and keeps several large sprinkling carts continually busy; with an electric light plant on the Westinghouse system of alternating currents, capable not only of thoroughly lighting the whole city but of furnishing the power for running an electric railway, for which the charter has already been granted by the City Council, and a large sum of money put up as a forfeiture by the company that accepted it....

I was witness of all this magical municipal development and could scarcely realize the miracle that was unfolding before me. There was no pretense that any person was there except for his individual self-interest; but the energy that the individual members of the community displayed, each for himself, resulted in the greatest benefit for the community as a whole. The wealth-creating force that was displayed in the building up of Guthrie cannot be better illustrated than in the fact that lots which had no value prior to April 22 sold in the center of the business movement as high as $500 within a week thereafter, and a number changed hands before the expiration of the first month for $1,500 each; while to my own knowledge a few sold, before sixty days had elapsed, for prices ranging from $1,700 to $5,000 per lot of 25 by 140 feet.

WILLIAM A. PEFFER: THE RISE OF FARMER ORGANIZATIONS (1891)

Source: *The Farmer's Side*, New York, 1891, pp. 148–161.

THE GRANGE

The Patrons of Husbandry, commonly known as the Grange, began their organization about twenty-four years ago in the city of Washington. The Grange grew rapidly about nine years, then quite as rapidly for a time receded from view; but in the meantime it had accomplished a noble work, much wider in its scope and grander in its proportions than people generally have ever been willing to admit. From the Grange came what is known as the "Granger" railroad legislation, the establishment in our laws of the principle that transportation belongs to the people, that it is a matter for the people themselves to manage in their own way, and that the Congress of the United States, under authority vested in that body by the Constitution, is authorized and empowered to regulate commerce among the several states as well as with foreign nations. That principle, once advocated and urged by the Grange, finally became permanently ingrafted in our laws.

Then came the Interstate Commerce Commission; that was another outcome of the Grange movement. Opposition to conspiracies of wealth against the rights of farmers—of labor in general, but of farmers in particular—was among the first and best works of the Grange. The footprints of that first and best organization of farmers ever effected up to that time—are seen plainly in much of the legislation of this country during the last twenty years. Grange influence revived in recent years, and is again growing. It is now one of the most earnest, active, and efficient agencies in the agitation of measures in the interest of agriculture. It lacks but one element of strength, and that will come in due time—namely, the uniting with other bodies of organized farmers in one great political movement to enforce themselves what they have long been trying ineffectually to enforce through their separate party organizations—the dethronement of the money power.

Aside from the political influence of the Grange, it has been a powerful factor in the social development of farmers. Go into a Grange neighborhood any place where the members have maintained their organization during all the troublesome, trying years that followed their first organization, and you find a neighborhood of thrifty, intelligent, well-advanced farmers, their wives and daughters enjoying all of the comforts and conveniences which have been brought into use through the multiplication of inventions for the saving of labor and the production of wealth. Their meetings have been schools in which the best sort of education comes; and now the Grange as a body is one of the most fruitful social institutions in the country. As fast as its members see their way clear to a union with their fellow farmers generally for political purposes, they will have accomplished a grand mission, and they will finally come to that.

THE FARMERS' ALLIANCE

The Farmers' Alliance is a body in many respects quite similar to that of the Grange. In both bodies women are equal with men in all of the privileges of the association. They are fast training women in channels of political thought. Many of the best essays and addresses read and delivered in their meetings are prepared by women, and it is beginning to dawn upon the minds of men long encrusted by custom and usage that the women who were chosen in early life as partners and companions—women who first became wives and then mothers and guardians of the best families upon earth, women who have nurtured children and trained them up to useful manhood and womanhood, looked after their interests when the days of childhood were numbered, and never forgot them "even until death"—these same women, who of all persons have a fonder attachment, a warmer affection, and a deeper love for their children, in the midst of mature life as well as in childhood, are quite as capable of looking after the interests of men and women when they are grown as while they are prattling infants about the playgrounds of the old homestead.

These social bodies of farmers, where men and women are at last made equal in public affairs, even though to a limited degree, are fast, very fast, educating the rural mind to the belief that women are as necessary in public affairs as they are in private affairs. Their influence is constantly growing stronger as the years come and go, and, strange as it may seem to some persons, they are losing none of their womanhood, but are constantly adding graces to lives already beautiful and useful.

The Farmers' Alliance was organized primarily—just as the Grange had been—for social purposes; but yet immediately in connection with its inception was an effort to defeat the absorption of state lands of Texas by speculators. One great object of the association was to save the public lands for the people. It has always been a leading idea among farmers that the public lands ought to be saved for homes for the people. They foresaw what the end would be in case speculators, whether individual or corporate, were allowed to monopolize the land. In time, settlers would be required to pay exorbitant prices for what they are entitled to at cost. The Homestead Law embodies the true theory of government disposition of the public lands. They belong to the people, in the right of the people.

Whatever they cost in money, if anything, was paid by the money of the people through a system of taxation, which was supposed to be just, bearing equally, as far as possible, upon all classes and conditions of the people. It was, as the farmers believed, a stupendous wrong inflicted upon the people of the country generally when lands were given away in immense quantities to corporations. All of that was so much money thrown into the coffers of rich men and wealthy corporations, and taken away from the poor. And now that our public lands are so much curtailed as that there is hardly room enough in fertile areas left to locate a single homestead, a great question comes up of taxing the people to inaugurate a general system of irrigation to reclaim arid lands, and to supply the demand for homes by increasing the productiveness of the public lands which are yet left for the use of the people; and this idea of "land for the landless and homes for the homeless"—once so noisy a party war cry—will again be made part of the platform of a national party which will rise into view within the next year or two.

The Farmers' Alliance is in two bodies now. One was begun in Texas about the year 1875; it is known as the "Southern Alliance." It has absorbed the "Farmers' Union" of Louisiana, the "Agricultural Wheel" of Arkansas, and some other local organizations of farmers in different parts of the Southern states, with Kansas,

Missouri, and Kentucky. It has a very large membership in Iowa, Ohio, and New York, and is spreading into all the other states. Thirty-five states now have organized alliances. While the body is strongest in Southern states, if its growth in the Northern and Western states continues to be as rapid the next year or two as it has been in the last two years, it will soon have a large membership in every state in the Union.

Its principles, socially and politically, are almost exactly the same as those taught by the Grange; namely, good fellowship and obliteration of sectional prejudices, a nationalizing of the people, a spirit of friendly feeling among the masses, abandonment of old issues, with the discussion of new problems of the present and the future, all based upon the fundamental idea which angels sang to shepherds when the Babe of Bethlehem was born—"Peace on earth, goodwill toward men." The "Southern Alliance," as it is commonly called by outsiders, is the "Farmers' Alliance and Industrial Union"; it is built upon principles broad and deep as humanity.

NATIONAL FARMERS' ALLIANCE

Then there is another body, known as the National Farmers' Alliance. It originated about the year 1877 in Illinois. It differs from the Southern Alliance practically only in this, that the Southern Alliance has a "secret work"; it transacts all of its business with closed doors; the members know one another outside as well as inside by means of "grips" and "passwords," just as Masons and Odd Fellows do. This is true likewise of the Grange. The National Farmers' Alliance, commonly known as the Northern Alliance, transacts its business openly, the same as any ordinary public assembly. The objects and aims of both bodies are practically the same—opposition to all private monopolies and the better dispensing of justice among the people. One of the tenets of all these organizations is "equal rights to all, special privileges to none."

FARMERS' MUTUAL BENEFIT ASSOCIATION

There is another rapidly growing body of farmers. It took form in the southern part of Illinois about four years ago. It is known as the Farmers' Mutual Benefit Association, with objects the same as the other bodies before named. It, too, has a secret work, but it differs from the Alliance and the Grange in that it does not admit women to membership; that will doubtless come later, for it seems that no considerable body of men in the discussion of matters which are largely social to begin with can very well get along without the help of women, who have been so serviceable to them in their home life.

There is a considerable number of other local bodies of farmers, as the Farmers' League, the Farmers' Union, the Farmers' Protective Association, Anti-Monopoly League, etc. These are mostly in Ohio and states to the eastward. The difference between the Alliance and other bodies of farmers named is about this: The Alliance is more aggressive along political lines than any of the others, and the Alliance has taken more advanced grounds in favor of independent political action. Alliance men and women in very large numbers have come to the conclusion that they have exhausted all of their means for effecting, through the agency of the old political parties, the needed changes in our legislation and customs.

THE KANSAS MOVEMENT

The lesson learned by the movement of Alliance men in Kansas in 1890 has been one of very great profit to the brethren in other parts of the country. It was discovered in Kansas that the party machinery was so completely in the hands of a few men as to make the party's policy simply what was dictated by the little circle of leaders, and it was evident that they were completely wedded to the power which has been absorbing the substance of the toilers. Kansas is an agricultural state, one of the most beautiful regions under heaven; with soil rich as any that the sun shines upon; with a climate salubrious; with an atmosphere balmy; with bright skies bending over a landscape delightful in its magnificent proportions; peopled by a rugged yeomanry—industrious, enterprising, sober, intelligent—a body of men and women unsurpassed anywhere in disposition to move forward

and upward; men and women who in less than the period of a generation have built an empire, have produced 50 million bushels of wheat and 250 million bushels of corn in one year, have opened 200,000 farms, have built 9,000 miles of railroad and 8,000 schoolhouses.

And the farmers of that state came to the conclusion that they were entitled to at least a fair share in the benefits of legislation. They found, however, that it was practically impossible to control the course of political parties, for the reason that the machinery was in the hands of men living in the towns, and connected in one way or another, to a greater or less degree, with railroads and with corporations engaged in the business of lending money for people in the East, deeply immersed in real-estate transactions, and in one way or another interested in matters that were directly and continually and powerfully in opposition to the interests of the farmers.

Looking the situation over carefully and deliberately, they came to the conclusion that the best way out of their troubles was through an independent political movement; so the Alliance submitted that proposition to their fellow workers inside and outside of the Alliance, to members of the Grange and of the Farmers' Mutual Benefit Association, to the Knights of Labor, to the Federation of Labor, and to other workers in different departments. The result was the formation of a political party known locally as the People's Party; and when the votes were counted after election day it appeared that the party was made up about as follows: Republicans, 45,000 voters; Democrats, 35,000 voters; Union-Labor men, 33,000 voters; Prohibitionists, 2,000 voters—making a total vote of 115,000.

The political complexion of the state was changed in six months to the extent of 100,000 votes. At the election in 1888 the Republican majority over all opposition was about 42,000 votes; at the election in 1890 that party fell short of a majority sixty-odd thousand votes. The People's Party in Kansas elected one state officer; attorney general; 5 out of the 7 members of Congress; 95 of the 125 members of the Lower House of the legislature (the senators elected in 1888 holding over to 1892); and secured the election of a United States senator on the 28th day of January following....

THE CINCINNATI CONFERENCE

The result in Kansas encouraged farmers in other states, and soon a movement was set on foot looking to the organization of an independent political movement covering the whole country. The first step in that direction was the National Union Conference, held at Cincinnati, May 19, 1891, composed of nearly 1,500 delegates representing thirty-two states and two territories—Alabama, Arkansas, California, Colorado, Connecticut, Florida, Illinois, Indiana, Iowa, Kansas, Kentucky, Louisiana, Maine, Massachusetts, Michigan, Minnesota, Missouri, Nebraska, New York, North Carolina, North Dakota, Ohio, Pennsylvania, Rhode Island, South Carolina, South Dakota, Tennessee, Texas, Washington, West Virginia, Wisconsin, Wyoming, Oklahoma, and District of Columbia.

A National Central Committee was appointed and arrangements made for a general union of all the industrial forces of the country in a convention in 1892 for the purpose of completing organization and putting a national ticket in the field.

JAMES LAURENCE LAUGHLIN: AGAINST FREE COINAGE OF SILVER (1895)

Source: *Facts About Money*, Chicago, 1895, pp. 223–238.

Money is used as a common denominator to which other things are referred for comparison. In order to compare goods with money, there is no more need of as many pieces of money as there are articles to be compared than there is of having a quart cup for every quart of milk in existence, or of having a yardstick in a dry goods store for every yard of cloth on the shelf. The idea that it is necessary to multiply the measurements of value is absurd; but it is of the foremost importance that the measure of values should not be tampered with and should not be changed by legislation to the damage of all transactions based upon it. Right here is the whole secret of the opposition to silver as money. Silver has lost its stability of value. It is no better than any ordinary metal for stability. The action of India in June 1893 sends it down 20 percent. The mere rumor of the Chinese indemnity sends it up 10 percent.

The greater or less quantity of money there is roaming about in circulation is no reason why anyone gets more of it. Money, like property, is parted with for a consideration. No matter how many more coins there are coming from the mint under free coinage and going into the vaults of the banks to the credit of the mine owners who own the bullion, there are no more coins in the pockets of Weary Waggles, who is cooling his heels on the sidewalk outside the bank.

The increased number of handsome horses and carriages on Michigan Avenue does not imply that I can get them if I have not the wealth to purchase them with. I must produce, work, turn out goods, and labor. I must get gold or silver or something equivalent to the value of the goods, and in that way I shall get them and in no other way. There is no way of getting rich by short cuts or by legislation or by merely increasing the means of exchanging goods, when goods themselves are the principal thing.

Money is the only machine by which goods are exchanged against one another. No matter how valuable, it is not wanted for itself. It is only a means to an end, like a bridge over a river. Do you suppose that the farmers of this country really believe that with each ton of silver taken out of the mines by the silver lawmaker in the Senate that there are created bushels of wheat and bushels of corn and barrels of mess pork? The silver belongs to the mine owners. How will it get into our pockets or the pockets of anyone else? Do we insult anyone's penetration by supposing that the congressional silver kings are going coaching about the country distributing their money for nothing? Our farmers are no fools. They know they can get more money only by producing more commodities to be exchanged for it and for those commodities they want as good money as any other men in the country have got....

As free coinage of silver would inevitably result in a rise of prices, it would immediately result in the fall of wages. Its first effect would be to diminish the purchasing power of all our wages. The man who gets $500 or $1,000 a year as a fixed rate of wages or salary will find he could buy just half as much as now. Yes, but someone will say, the employer will raise his wages. Now, will he? But the facts on that point are clear and indisputable. It has been one of the undisputed facts of history that, when prices rise, the wages of labor are the last to advance; and when prices fall, the wages of labor are the first to decline. Free coinage of silver would make all the articles of the laborer's consumption cost him 100 percent more unless he can get a rise in his wages by dint of strikes and quarrels and all the consequent dissatisfaction arising from friction between the employer and employee. He would be able to buy only one-half as many articles of daily consumption as he had before.

In short, a rise of prices necessarily results in a diminution of the enjoyments of the laboring class until they can force the employers, through a long process of agitation, to make an increase in their wages. Are we willing to sacrifice the interests of the laboring classes to the demands of certain owners of silver mines who hope to hoodwink the people with the cry of more money? This would be, clearly enough, distinct and serious damage.

The damage runs in other directions, however. The proposal to adopt a depreciated standard of value is simply an attempt to transfer from the great mass of the community who have been provident, industrious, and successful, a portion of their savings and gains into the pockets of those who have been idle, extravagant, or unfortunate. The provision which has been made for old age, for sickness, for death, for widows and orphans, or by insurance will be depreciated in the same ratio. No invasion of hostile armies, burning and destroying as they advance, could by any possibility equal the desolation and ruin which would thus be forced upon the great mass of the American people.

Such a depreciation, however—as all experience and history has shown—does not fall alike upon the shrewd and the unsophisticated. The shrewd ones, the bankers, etc., will be easily able to take care of themselves; while we plain people will be robbed of our hard-won earnings without any hope of compensation.

Free coinage of silver at 16:1 would injure all those who wish to borrow because it would frighten lenders and make them unwilling to lend except at high rates of interest. Moreover, since the average term of mortgages, in general, is not over five or six years, present indebtedness of this kind does not run back to 1873. Free coinage is essentially dishonest.

If I have saved painfully $1,000 by many years of sacrifice and lend it to B on a mortgage; then, if B urges legislation by which he can pay me back in a cheaper money worth one-half of what he got from me, do you suppose I would ever again lend to B or renew my mortgage? If I had pinched or saved, gone without a new over-coat, or used a shabby parlor carpet in order to save something and invest it for my child, and then I gave it over to B, who has had the spending of it, isn't it fair and square that I should have back again what I gave? If B had the enjoyment from spending it, he is not thereby absolved from paying it back. No trick or sophistry can make the scaling of this debt to me anything but dishonesty and cheating.

Any state that enacts laws whereby debts can be scaled signs its own commercial doom. No one will invest where he foresees repudiation; loans cannot be made except at rates so high as to pay for the risks of loss. Cheating is bad business policy for man or state....

The Sherman Act of July 4, 1890, unless it had been repealed, would have brought us to the silver standard as it was. The mere suspicion of it struck a blow at our measure of value, brought on a panic, made prices uncertain, and caused doubts as to future plans in every factory and shop in the land. Those who have silver mines, and who can by their wealth control political parties and legislatures, who make the very seat of our national government their private offices, and actually turn the national Senate into a bureau for bulling the prices of their product—to those men we say, beware.

Those of us who belong to the rank of plain citizens, who are thinking only of the country as a whole, who believe in the honesty and intelligence of the people, hold that when a question of right or wrong is presented in a campaign of education the people will decide for right and for justice. We cannot believe that a special interest, led by millionaires, can go on unchecked in their plan of sacrificing the taxpayers in order to heap up riches, especially when this is done on the most fallacious of all economic grounds— grounds which have been proved wrong by the experience of every country of modern times.

How long will it take to convince every man in the land that conditions of prosperity are those in which the honest man can best meet and pay his obligations? Unless a debtor can get employment or find a market for his goods, how can he pay interest or principal? Now, if tampering with the standard in the terms of which all transactions are drawn, all contracts made, all goods bought and sold brings industrial paralysis because no one knows what will happen ten days ahead, and no one will go on making goods for a changing market, except at ruinous profits, it is to the interest of every laborer, every debtor, every honest

man, is it not, to keep and maintain the value of the standard so far as that may be done? The debtor will be no better off by free coinage. Even if we had it—which we never will—every lender would insert the gold clause in the contract....

Is it true that, even laying aside all honor and justice, resorting to a single silver standard depreciated 50 percent, the debtor will sell his goods at 100 percent more, and the more easily pay off his debts? By no means. That is the most superficial of all views. Trickery is always sure to follow those who resort to it. And I do not myself feel it necessary only to appeal to the selfish motives of the American people. I for one am ready to appeal to that integrity, that sense of honor, and that uprightness in the American people which, whenever it has been appealed to, has decided rightly upon these great questions of justice.

In conclusion, gentlemen, extraordinary as is the proposal for free coinage, it is in truth only a huge deceit. It was born in the private offices of the silver kings, nursed at the hands of speculators, clothed in economic error, fed on boodle, exercised in the lobby of Congress, and as sure as there is honesty and truth in the American heart it will die young and be buried in the same ignominious grave wherein lies the now-forgotten infant once famous as the rag baby.

Free coinage is greenbackism galvanized into life. That heresy in its old form of a demand for more money has already been laid low. It will not long deceive us in its new form of a demand for more silver, or for silver fiatism. Nor in any other respect is it what it presumes to be. It is not a proposition for bimetallism. It is a wild leap in the dark for silver mono-metallism. Under the cry for more money are veiled the plans of a daring syndicate of mine owners and speculators who have hoodwinked the people in certain parts of the country and who, while deluding them with a specious argument for more money, are laughing in their sleeves at a constituency so easily gulled.

JACOB S. COXEY: BUSINESS DEPRESSION AND PUBLIC WORKS (1894)

Source: *Henry Vincent, The Story of the Commonweal,* Chicago, 1894, pp. 51–53.

THE BILL...TO BUILD GOOD ROADS...

Section 1. Be it enacted by the Senate and House of Representatives in Congress assembled, that the secretary of the Treasury of the United States is hereby authorized and instructed to have engraved and printed, immediately after the passage of this bill, $500 million of Treasury notes, a legal tender for all debts, public and private, said notes to be in denominations of $1, $2, $5, and $10; and to be placed in a fund to be known as the General County Road Fund System of the United States, and to be expended solely for said purpose.

Section 2. And be it further enacted, that it shall be the duty of the secretary of war to take charge of the construction of the said General County Road System in the United States, and said construction to commence as soon as the secretary of the Treasury shall inform the secretary of war that the said fund is available, which shall not be later than ———; when it shall be the duty of the secretary of war to inaugurate the work and expend the sum of $20 million per month, pro rata, with the number of miles of roads in each state and territory in the United States.

Section 3. Be it further enacted, that all labor other than that of the secretary of war, "whose compensations are already fixed by law," shall be paid by the day, and that the rate be not less than $1.50 per day for common labor and $3.50 per day for team and labor; and that eight hours per day shall constitute a day's labor under the provisions of this bill.

THE NONINTEREST BEARING BOND BILL...

Be it enacted by the Senate and House of Representatives in Congress assembled, that whenever any state, territory, county, township, municipality, or incorporated town or village deem it necessary to make any public improvements, they shall deposit with the secretary of the Treasury of the United States a noninterest bearing, twenty-five-year bond, not to exceed one-half the assessed valuation of the property in said state, territory, county, township, municipality, or incorporated town or village, and said bond to be retired at the rate of 4 percent per annum.

Whenever the foregoing section of this act has been complied with, it shall be mandatory upon the secretary of the Treasury of the United States to have engraved and printed Treasury notes in the denominations of $1, $2, $5, $10, and $20 each, which shall be a full legal tender for all debts, public and private, to the face value of said bond; and deliver to said state, territory, county, township, municipality, or incorporated town or village 99 percent of said notes and retain 1 percent for expense of engraving and printing same.

WILLIAM JENNINGS BRYAN: THE CROSS OF GOLD (1896)

Source: *Official Proceedings of the Democratic National Convention Held in Chicago, Ill., July 7, 8, 9, 10, and 11, 1896, Logansport, Ind., 1896, pp. 226–234.*

I would be presumptuous, indeed, to present myself against the distinguished gentlemen to whom you have listened if this were but a measuring of ability; but this is not a contest among persons. The humblest citizen in all the land when clad in armor of a righteous cause is stronger than all the whole hosts of error that they can bring. I come to speak to you in defense of a cause as holy as the cause of liberty—the cause of humanity. When this debate is concluded, a motion will be made to lay upon the table the resolution offered in commendation of the administration and also the resolution in condemnation of the administration. I shall object to bringing this question down to a level of persons. The individual is but an atom; he is born, he acts, he dies; but principles are eternal; and this has been a contest of principle.

Never before in the history of this country has there been witnessed such a contest as that through which we have passed. Never before in the history of American politics has a great issue been fought out as this issue has been by the voters themselves.

On the 4th of March, 1895, a few Democrats, most of them members of Congress, issued an address to the Democrats of the nation asserting that the money question was the paramount issue of the hour; asserting also the right of a majority of the Democratic Party to control the position of the party on this paramount issue; concluding with the request that all believers in free coinage of silver in the Democratic Party should organize and take charge of and control the policy of the Democratic Party. Three months later, at Memphis, an organization was perfected, and the silver Democrats went forth openly and boldly and courageously proclaiming their belief and declaring that if successful they would crystallize in a platform the declaration which they had made; and then began the conflict with a zeal approaching the zeal which inspired the crusaders who followed Peter the Hermit. Our silver Democrats went forth from victory unto victory, until they are assembled now, not to discuss, not to debate, but to enter up the judgment rendered by the plain people of this country.

But in this contest, brother has been arrayed against brother, and father against son. The warmest ties of love and acquaintance and association have been disregarded. Old leaders have been cast aside when they refused to give expression to the sentiments of those whom they would lead, and new leaders have sprung up to give direction to this cause of freedom. Thus has the contest been waged, and we have assembled here under as binding and solemn instructions as were ever fastened upon the representatives of a people.

We do not come as individuals. Why, as individuals we might have been glad to compliment the gentleman from New York [Senator Hill], but we knew that the people for whom we speak would never be willing to put him in a position where he could thwart the will of the Democratic Party. I say it was not a question of persons; it was a question of principle; and it is not with gladness, my friends, that we find ourselves brought into conflict with those who are now arrayed on the other side. The gentleman who just preceded me [Governor Russell] spoke of the old state of Massachusetts. Let me assure him that not one person in all this convention entertains the least hostility to the people of the state of Massachusetts.

But we stand here representing people who are the equals before the law of the largest cities in the state of Massachusetts. When you come before us and tell us that we shall disturb your business interests, we reply that you have disturbed our business interests by your action. We say to you that you have made too limited in its application the definition of a businessman. The man who is employed for wages is as much a businessman as his employer. The attorney in a country town is as much a businessman as the corporation counsel in a great metropolis. The merchant at the crossroads store is as much a businessman as the merchant of New York. The farmer who goes forth in the morning and toils all day, begins in the spring and toils all summer, and by the application of brain and muscle to the natural resources of this country creates wealth, is as much a businessman as the man who goes upon the Board of Trade and bets upon the price of grain. The miners who go 1,000 feet into the earth or climb 2,000 feet upon the cliffs and bring forth from their hiding places the precious metals to be poured in the channels of trade are as much businessmen as the few financial magnates who in a backroom corner the money of the world.

We come to speak for this broader class of businessmen. Ah, my friends, we say not one word against those who live upon the Atlantic Coast; but those hardy pioneers who braved all the dangers of the wilderness, who have made the desert to blossom as the rose—those pioneers away out there, rearing their children near to nature's heart, where they can mingle their voices with the voices of the birds—out there where they have erected schoolhouses for the education of their children and churches where they praise their Creator, and the cemeteries where sleep the ashes of their dead—are as deserving of the consideration of this party as any people in this country.

It is for these that we speak. We do not come as aggressors. Our war is not a war of conquest. We are fighting in the defense of our homes, our families, and posterity. We have petitioned, and our petitions have been scorned. We have entreated, and our entreaties have been disregarded. We have begged, and they have mocked when our calamity came.

We beg no longer; we entreat no more; we petition no more. We defy them!

The gentleman from Wisconsin has said he fears a Robespierre. My friend, in this land of the free you need fear no tyrant who will spring up from among the people. What we need is an Andrew Jackson to stand as Jackson stood, against the encroachments of aggregated wealth.

They tell us that this platform was made to catch votes. We reply to them that changing conditions make new issues; that the principles upon which rest Democracy are as everlasting as the hills; but that they must be applied to new conditions as they arise. Conditions have arisen and we are attempting to meet those conditions. They tell us that the income tax ought not to be brought in here; that is not a new idea. They criticize us for our criticism of the Supreme Court of the United States. My friends, we have made no criticism. We have simply called attention to what you know. If you want criticisms, read the dissenting opinions of the Court. That will give you criticisms.

They say we passed an unconstitutional law. I deny it. The income tax was not unconstitutional when it was passed. It was not unconstitutional when it went before the Supreme Court for the first time. It did not become unconstitutional until one judge changed his mind; and we cannot be expected to know when a judge will change his mind.

The income tax is a just law. It simply intends to put the burdens of government justly upon the backs of the people. I am in favor of an income tax. When I find a man who is not willing to pay his share of the burden of the government which protects him, I find a man who is unworthy to enjoy the blessings of a government like ours.

He says that we are opposing the national bank currency. It is true. If you will read what Thomas Benton said, you will find that he said that in searching history he could find but one parallel to Andrew Jackson. That was Cicero, who destroyed the conspiracies of Cataline and saved Rome. He did for Rome what Jackson did when he destroyed the bank conspiracy and saved America.

We say in our platform that we believe that the right to coin money and issue money is a function of government. We believe it. We believe it is a part of sovereignty and can no more with safety be delegated to private individuals than can the power to make penal statutes or levy laws for taxation.

Mr. Jefferson, who was once regarded as good Democratic authority, seems to have a different opinion from the gentleman who has addressed us on the part of the minority. Those who are opposed to this proposition tell us that the issue of paper money is a function of the bank and that the government ought to go out of the banking business. I stand with Jefferson rather than with them, and tell them, as he did, that the issue of money is a function of the government and that the banks should go out of the governing business.

They complain about the plank which declares against the life tenure in office. They have tried to strain it to mean that which it does not mean. What we oppose in that plank is the life tenure that is being built up in Washington which establishes an officeholding class and excludes from participation in the benefits the humbler members of our society....

Let me call attention to two or three great things. The gentleman from New York says that he will propose an amendment providing that this change in our law shall not affect contracts which, according to the present laws, are made payable in gold. But if he means to say that we cannot change our monetary system without protecting those who have loaned money before the change was made, I want to ask him where, in law or in morals, he can find authority for not protecting the debtors when the act of 1873 was passed when he now insists that we must protect the creditor. He says

he also wants to amend this platform so as to provide that if we fail to maintain the parity within a year that we will then suspend the coinage of silver. We reply that when we advocate a thing which we believe will be successful we are not compelled to raise a doubt as to our own sincerity by trying to show what we will do if we are wrong.

I ask him, if he will apply his logic to us, why he does not apply it to himself. He says that he wants this country to try to secure an international agreement. Why doesn't he tell us what he is going to do if they fail to secure an international agreement. There is more reason for him to do that than for us to expect to fail to maintain the parity. They have tried for thirty years—thirty years—to secure an international agreement, and those are waiting for it most patiently who don't want it at all.

Now, my friends, let me come to the great paramount issue. If they ask us here why it is we say more on the money question than we say upon the tariff question, I reply that if protection has slain its thousands the gold standard has slain its tens of thousands. If they ask us why we did not embody all these things in our platform which we believe, we reply to them that when we have restored the money of the Constitution, all other necessary reforms will be possible, and that until that is done there is no reform that can be accomplished.

Why is it that within three months such a change has come over the sentiments of the country? Three months ago, when it was confidently asserted that those who believed in the gold standard would frame our platforms and nominate our candidates, even the advocates of the gold standard did not think that we could elect a President; but they had good reasons for the suspicion, because there is scarcely a state here today asking for the gold standard that is not within the absolute control of the Republican Party.

But note the change. Mr. McKinley was nominated at St. Louis upon a platform that declared for the maintenance of the gold standard until it should be changed into bimetallism by an international agreement. Mr. McKinley was the most popular man among the Republicans and everybody three months ago in the Republican Party prophesied his election. How is it today? Why, that man who used to boast that he looked like Napoleon, that man shudders today when he thinks that he was nominated on the anniversary of the Battle of Waterloo. Not only that, but as he listens he can hear with ever increasing distinctness the sound of the waves as they beat upon the lonely shores of St. Helena.

Why this change? Ah, my friends, is not the change evident to anyone who will look at the matter? It is because no private character, however pure, no personal popularity, however great, can protect from the avenging wrath of an indignant people the man who will either declare that he is in favor of fastening the gold standard upon this people, or who is willing

to surrender the right of self-government and place legislative control in the hands of foreign potentates and powers....

We go forth confident that we shall win. Why? Because upon the paramount issue in this campaign there is not a spot of ground upon which the enemy will dare to challenge battle. Why, if they tell us that the gold standard is a good thing, we point to their platform and tell them that their platform pledges the party to get rid of a gold standard and substitute bimetallism. If the gold standard is a good thing, why try to get rid of it? If the gold standard, and I might call your attention to the fact that some of the very people who are in this convention today and who tell you that we ought to declare in favor of international bimetallism and thereby declare that the gold standard is wrong and that the principles of bimetallism are better—these very people four months ago were open and avowed advocates of the gold standard and telling us that we could not legislate two metals together even with all the world.

I want to suggest this truth, that if the gold standard is a good thing we ought to declare in favor of its retention and not in favor of abandoning it; and if the gold standard is a bad thing, why should we wait until some other nations are willing to help us to let it go?

Here is the line of battle. We care not upon which issue they force the fight. We are prepared to meet them on either issue or on both. If they tell us that the gold standard is the standard of civilization, we reply to them that this, the most enlightened of all nations of the earth, has never declared for a gold standard, and both the parties this year are declaring against it. If the gold standard is the standard of civilization, why, my friends, should we not have it? So if they come to meet us on that, we can present the history of our nation. More than that, we can tell them this, that they will search the pages of history in vain to find a single instance in which the common people of any land ever declared themselves in favor of a gold standard. They can find where the holders of fixed investments have.

Mr. Carlisle said in 1878 that this was a struggle between the idle holders of idle capital and the struggling masses who produce the wealth and pay the taxes of the country; and my friends, it is simply a question that we shall decide upon which side shall the Democratic Party fight. Upon the side of the idle holders of idle capital, or upon the side of the struggling masses? That is the question that the party must answer first; and then it must be answered by each individual hereafter. The sympathies of the Democratic Party, as described by the platform, are on the side of the struggling masses, who have ever been the foundation of the Democratic Party.

There are two ideas of government. There are those who believe that if you just legislate to make the well-to-do prosperous that their prosperity will leak through on those below. The Democratic idea has been that if you legislate to make the masses prosperous their prosperity will find its way up and through every class that rests upon it.

You come to us and tell us that the great cities are in favor of the gold standard. I tell you that the great cities rest upon these broad and fertile prairies. Burn down your cities and leave our farms, and your cities will spring up again as if by magic. But destroy our farms and the grass will grow in the streets of every city in this country.

My friends, we shall declare that this nation is able to legislate for its own people on every question without waiting for the aid or consent of any other nation on earth, and upon that issue we expect to carry every single state in this Union.

I shall not slander the fair state of Massachusetts nor the state of New York by saying that when its citizens are confronted with the proposition, "Is this nation able to attend to its own business?"—I will not slander either one by saying that the people of those states will declare our helpless impotency as a nation to attend to our own business. It is the issue of 1776 over again. Our ancestors, when but 3 million, had the courage to declare their political independence of every other nation upon earth. Shall we, their descendants, when we have grown to 70 million, declare that we are less independent than our forefathers? No, my friends, it will never be the judgment of this people. Therefore, we care not upon what lines the battle is fought.

If they say bimetallism is good but we cannot have it till some nation helps us, we reply that, instead of having a gold standard because England has, we shall restore bimetallism, and then let England have bimetallism because the United States have.

If they dare to come out and in the open defend the gold standard as a good thing, we shall fight them to the uttermost, having behind us the producing masses of the nation and the world. Having behind us the commercial interests and the laboring interests and all the toiling masses, we shall answer their demands for a gold standard by saying to them, you shall not press down upon the brow of labor this crown of thorns. You shall not crucify mankind upon a cross of gold.

assay Analysis to determine the presence, absence, or quantity of one or more components (often ores).

bimettalism The use of two metals (as gold and silver) jointly as a monetary standard with both constituting legal tender at a predetermined ratio.

bullion Uncoined gold or silver in bars or ingots.

coolie Slang term for an unskilled labourer or porter, usually in or from East Asia, hired for low or subsistence wages.

demagogue A leader who makes use of popular prejudices and false claims and promises in order to gain power.

extortion The act of obtaining usually money or property from a person by force, intimidation, or undue or illegal power.

laissez-faire A doctrine opposing governmental interference in economic affairs beyond the minimum necessary for the maintenance of peace and property rights.

lien A charge upon real or personal property for the satisfaction of some debt or duty ordinarily arising by operation of law.

monopoly Exclusive ownership through legal privilege, command of supply, or concerted action.

muckraker One who searches out and publicly exposes real or apparent misconduct of a prominent individual or business.

parity Quality or state of being equal, especially equality of purchasing power.

pogrom An organized massacre of helpless people; specifically, such a massacre of Jews.

prima facie On the first appearance.

proletarian Of or relating to the class of industrial workers who lack their own means of production and hence sell their labour to live.

quorum The number (as a majority) of officers or members of a body that when duly assembled is legally competent to transact business.

remonstrate To present and urge reasons in opposition.

requisition The act of formally requiring or calling upon someone to perform an action.

salubrious Favourable to or promoting health or well-being.

slatternly Untidy and dirty through habitual neglect.

speculation Assumption of unusual business risk in hopes of obtaining commensurate gain.

squat To settle on public land under government regulation with the purpose of acquiring title.

tatterdemalion Ragged or disreputable in appearance.

trust A combination of firms or corporations formed by a legal agreement, especially one that reduces or threatens to reduce competition.

BIBLIOGRAPHY

NATIONAL EXPANSION

Walter Prescott Webb, *The Great Plains* (1931, reprinted 1981), is a scholarly classic; also useful are Ray Allen Billington and Martin Ridge, *Westward Expansion*, 5th ed. (1982); and Rodman W. Paul, *The Far West and the Great Plains in Transition, 1859–1900* (1988). Henry E. Fritz, *The Movement for Indian Assimilation, 1860–1890* (1963, reprinted 1981), traces the development of this policy after the Civil War. Studies of the occupation of the Plains by the farmers are Fred A. Shannon, *The Farmer's Last Frontier: Agriculture, 1860–1897* (1945, reprinted 1977); and Gilbert C. Fite, *The Farmers' Frontier, 1865–1900* (1966, reissued 1987).

INDUSTRIAL DEVELOPMENT

Glenn Porter, *The Rise of Big Business: 1860–1920* (2006); Richard Bensel, *The Political Economy of American Industrialization, 1877–1900* (2000); Edward C. Kirkland, *Industry Comes of Age* (1961); and Samuel P. Hays, *The Response to Industrialism, 1885–1914* (1957), offer a perceptive appraisals of the impact of business and industry on American life. Discussion of the trade unions during the second half of the 19th century is found in Norman J. Ware, *The Labor Movement in the United States, 1860–1895* (1929, reprinted 1964).

POLITICS

T. Jackson Lears, *Rebirth of a Nation: The Making of Modern America, 1877–1920* (2009); and Sean Dennis Cashman, *America in the Gilded Age: From the Death of Lincoln to the Rise of Theodore Roosevelt*, 3rd ed. (1993), provide overviews of the era. Leonard D. White, *The Republican Era, 1869–1901* (1958, reissued 1965), presents a careful and useful analysis. H. Wayne Morgan, *From Hayes to McKinley: National Party Politics, 1877–1896* (1969); and Harold U. Faulkner, *Politics, Reform, and Expansion, 1890–1900* (1959, reissued 1963), are still valuable. Studies of populism include Robert C. MacMath, *American Populism: A Social History, 1877–1898* (1993); John D. Hicks, *The Populist Revolt* (1931, reprinted 1981); and Lawrence Goodwyn, *Democratic Promise: The Populist Moment in America* (1976).